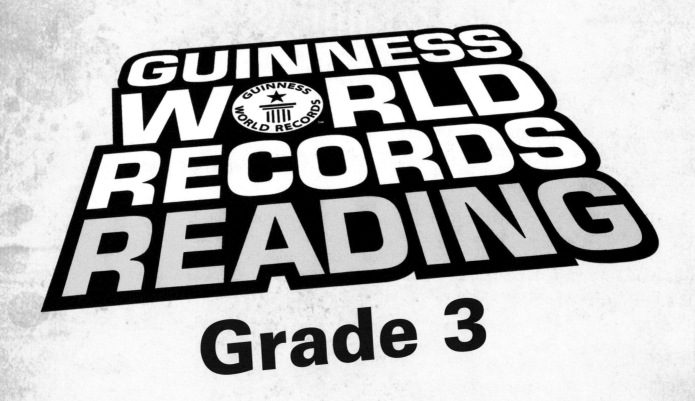

Grade 3

by Melissa & Henry Billings

Carson-Dellosa Publishing LLC
Greensboro, North Carolina

GUINNESS WORLD RECORDS™ DISCLAIMER: Guinness World Records Limited has a very thorough accreditation system for records verification. However, while every effort is made to ensure accuracy, Guinness World Records Limited cannot be held responsible for any errors contained in this work. Feedback from our readers on any point of accuracy is always welcomed.

SAFETY DISCLAIMER: Attempting to break records or set new records can be dangerous. Appropriate advice should be taken first, and all record attempts are undertaken entirely at the participant's risk. In no circumstances will Guinness World Records Limited or Carson-Dellosa Publishing LLC have any liability for death or injury suffered in any record attempts. Guinness World Records Limited has complete discretion over whether or not to include any particular records in the annual Guinness World Records book.

Due to the publication date, the facts and the figures contained in this book are current as of July 2010.

© 2011 Guinness World Records Limited

Visit Guinness World Records at www.guinnessworldrecords.com.

Credits

Content Editor: Ginny Swinson

Copy Editor: Karen Seberg

Layout and Cover Design: Van Harris

Carson-Dellosa Publishing LLC
PO Box 35665
Greensboro, NC 27425 USA
www.carsondellosa.com

ISBN 978-1-936024-05-6
045111151

TABLE OF CONTENTS

INTRODUCTION

Guinness World Records™ Reading gives students the opportunity to shatter their own records—reading records, that is! Just as ordinary people can become Guinness World Record holders, students can become world record readers when they experience the excitement of *Guinness World Records™ Reading*. Designed for struggling or reluctant readers, students on grade level, and high achievers, *Guinness World Records™ Reading* helps improve reading comprehension skills and motivates students to do their best.

What does it mean to be the best? Guinness World Record holders know! Some of them are people, such as the woman who ran a marathon on stilts. Some are animals, such as the goldfish that does six different tricks. Some record-holders are even igloos and paper dolls! In this book, more than 50 stories chronicle the triumphs of people, animals, nature, science, and technology. The feats and successes are thrilling, and the records will amaze and inspire readers of all ages.

4

IN THIS BOOK

Guinness World Records™ Reading is divided into five themed units, with each unit highlighting incredible achievements in a specific category. Some of the records are exciting, some are unsettling, and some of them are just plain unbelievable—but, they are all extraordinary!

In the first unit, discover **Amazing Animals**, big and small: Meet a tiny horse named Thumbelina, a spider the size of a dinner plate, an animal that can roll down a hand-cranked car window, and a rabbit with ears that drag on the floor. Who knew that rabbit ears could span the length of a yardstick?

In the next unit, explore records in **Engineering, Science & the Body**: Walk into an igloo large enough for 200 people, see a monster (truck, that is) as big as two elephants, check out a woman whose hair is three times the length of her body, and meet a boy with a 281-pound (127.5-kg) ball of plastic wrap! Absolutely record breaking!

Experience the intensity of our home planet in **Earth Extremes**: Meet a snowman so big that its buttons are truck tires, get lost in a prairie dog town with 400 million residents, and visit a plant that grows 32,000 tomatoes. If that's not extreme, then what is?

Game Time! is sure to get you moving: Ride a 36-foot-long (11-m-long) skateboard, build a house with 1,800 decks of cards, and hop on a speedy minibob sled going 97 miles (156 km) per hour. You'll be at the bottom of the hill before you know it!

Just when you think you have heard it all, **Wild, Wacky & Weird** proves you haven't: One record-breaker grew her fingernails to three feet (0.9 m) long, another balances car frames on his head, and yet another makes sandwiches with his feet. Wacky? The wackiest!

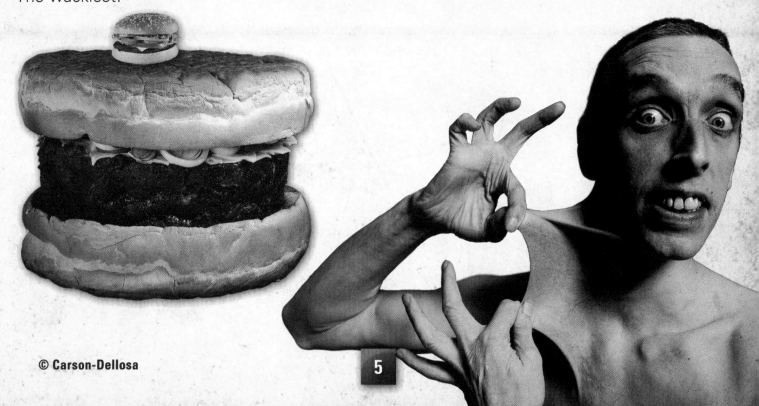

HOW THIS BOOK WORKS

Guinness World Records™ Reading provides parents and teachers with materials and experiences that make reading compelling and fun for students. The high-interest, grade-level-appropriate reading passages are based on actual Guinness World Records. More than 50 short passages offer subject matter that motivates and engages even the most reluctant students to read, write, and explore fascinating topics. Students will become world record readers as they absorb astounding content, expand their vocabulary, and add to their knowledge of unusual facts and inspiring people.

Refer to each themed unit to select subjects of specific interest to your students or choose subjects based on units within your curriculum. Use the matrix to identify the skills that each lesson targets. Achievement of each skill varies, depending on the depth of knowledge students demonstrate in their answers.

- Each passage about a Guinness World Record holder is followed by questions that target such basic skills as recalling, summarizing, understanding the main idea, making connections, and drawing conclusions.

- Questions progress in difficulty using Bloom's Taxonomy for ease of differentiating instruction and for focused practice on higher-level thinking skills, such as predicting, applying, and analyzing.

- Vocabulary questions of various contexts and formats revisit challenging and practical vocabulary words (boldfaced in each passage) by working with words, definitions, and usage.

- Extension activities or critical response questions complete each question page. Students will expand their knowledge and creativity with more than 100 of these bonus questions to choose from!

- Summarizing puzzles and games at the end of each unit monitor student comprehension and reinforce vocabulary with an array of fun and engaging formats.

ARE *YOU* THE NEXT WORLD RECORD-HOLDER?

Do you think that you have what it takes to break a Guinness World Record? You just might! With dedication, persistence, and an idea, anything is possible. If you have an idea and you are ready to commit, get your family's permission and then go for it! Who knows? Your name could be in next year's record book. How do you do it? Read on!

First, what kind of record would you like to break? Do you have a unique talent? Are you the only person able to do something? If your talent is interesting or exciting, you have a good chance!

Do you own a unique object? Is it the only object of its kind? If it's a record that someone can break, such as owning the cow with the longest horns, then you're on your way. Or, if you think that you're the youngest person to achieve a certain feat, Guinness World Records may be interested. Just make sure that the feat is of international interest and, of course, something that is legal to do at your age!

Are you thinking of being the first at something? That's the hardest record to achieve. "Firsts" have to be important enough to have historical or international significance, such as the First Woman to Walk to the North Pole.

Not sure which record to break? Are you interested in going for a record that is regularly broken? The DJ marathon and various mass participation events are the records broken most often.

When you've decided which record to break, complete the registration form on the Guinness World Records Web site. Then, submit an application. Your application will include your proposal for the record. You'll know in about four weeks if your proposal is accepted. If it is, you are ready to go! Make sure that you follow the guidelines carefully. You'll have to collect and submit evidence of your record. Now, all you have to do is break that record!

Did You Know?
Guinness World Records receives more than 60,000 inquiries every year from potential record-breakers. A total of 40,000 records are in the Guinness database.

SKILLS MATRIX

Page Number	Comprehension Strategies								Vocabulary Development			Higher Order Thinking Skills					
	Recalling	Activating Prior Knowledge	Making Connections	Summarizing	Understanding Main Idea	Monitoring Comprehension	Drawing Conclusions	Determining Fact vs. Opinion	Increasing Vocabulary	Using Context Clues	Word Study	Predicting	Application	Analysis	Synthesis	Evaluation	Critical Response
11	✔	✔	✔		✔	✔	✔		✔	✔			✔			✔	
13	✔	✔	✔			✔			✔	✔		✔	✔	✔			
15	✔	✔	✔			✔			✔								✔
17	✔	✔	✔						✔		✔		✔				
19	✔	✔	✔	✔	✔	✔			✔	✔			✔				
21	✔	✔	✔			✔	✔		✔	✔		✔	✔				✔
23	✔	✔	✔			✔	✔		✔	✔		✔	✔	✔			
25	✔	✔	✔			✔			✔	✔		✔	✔				
27	✔	✔	✔						✔	✔			✔	✔	✔		
29	✔	✔	✔			✔			✔				✔				
31		✔	✔		✔	✔			✔				✔				
33	✔	✔	✔			✔			✔	✔		✔	✔				✔
35	✔		✔	✔	✔	✔	✔		✔	✔			✔	✔			
36									✔								
37	✔				✔								✔				
39	✔	✔	✔		✔				✔	✔		✔	✔				
41	✔	✔	✔		✔	✔			✔			✔	✔				
43	✔		✔		✔		✔		✔	✔		✔	✔	✔			
45	✔	✔	✔		✔		✔		✔	✔		✔	✔	✔			
47	✔	✔	✔		✔				✔	✔			✔				✔
49	✔	✔	✔		✔		✔		✔	✔		✔	✔	✔	✔		
51	✔		✔	✔	✔	✔			✔	✔	✔		✔				
53	✔	✔	✔	✔		✔			✔				✔				
55	✔	✔	✔			✔	✔		✔	✔		✔	✔			✔	✔
56	✔								✔								
57	✔				✔								✔				
59	✔	✔	✔		✔	✔	✔		✔	✔		✔	✔	✔			
61	✔	✔	✔			✔			✔	✔			✔		✔		
63	✔	✔	✔		✔				✔	✔	✔		✔				
65	✔		✔			✔	✔		✔	✔						✔	✔
67	✔					✔	✔		✔	✔	✔	✔	✔	✔	✔	✔	
69	✔				✔				✔		✔		✔	✔		✔	✔

Page Number	Comprehension Strategies								Vocabulary Development			Higher Order Thinking Skills					
	Recalling	Activating Prior Knowledge	Making Connections	Summarizing	Understanding Main Idea	Monitoring Comprehension	Drawing Conclusions	Determining Fact vs. Opinion	Increasing Vocabulary	Using Context Clues	Word Study	Predicting	Application	Analysis	Synthesis	Evaluation	Critical Response
71	✔	✔	✔			✔	✔		✔	✔		✔		✔			
73	✔	✔	✔		✔	✔			✔	✔		✔	✔		✔		
75	✔	✔	✔		✔		✔		✔	✔		✔	✔				
77	✔	✔	✔		✔		✔		✔	✔		✔					✔
79	✔	✔	✔		✔	✔			✔	✔		✔	✔	✔			
80	✔								✔								
81	✔				✔												
83	✔	✔		✔					✔		✔			✔			
85	✔	✔	✔		✔	✔			✔	✔		✔		✔			✔
87	✔	✔	✔		✔		✔		✔	✔		✔	✔				
89	✔	✔			✔	✔	✔		✔		✔						✔
91	✔	✔	✔	✔	✔	✔			✔	✔			✔	✔			
93	✔		✔			✔	✔		✔				✔	✔			✔
95	✔	✔	✔		✔		✔		✔	✔				✔			
97	✔	✔	✔		✔	✔			✔	✔		✔	✔	✔			
99	✔	✔	✔		✔	✔			✔	✔			✔	✔			
100									✔								
101	✔				✔												
103	✔	✔	✔	✔	✔	✔	✔		✔	✔	✔	✔	✔				
105	✔	✔	✔		✔	✔			✔	✔			✔				
107	✔				✔	✔			✔	✔				✔			✔
109	✔	✔	✔		✔	✔	✔		✔	✔		✔	✔	✔	✔		
111	✔	✔	✔				✔		✔					✔			
113	✔	✔	✔		✔				✔	✔							
115	✔	✔				✔	✔		✔	✔			✔	✔			
117	✔	✔	✔			✔			✔	✔			✔	✔			
119	✔	✔	✔	✔	✔		✔		✔	✔				✔			
121	✔				✔	✔	✔		✔	✔							✔
123	✔	✔	✔		✔		✔		✔	✔		✔	✔				
124	✔				✔				✔					✔			
125	✔				✔									✔			

ROLL DOWN THAT WINDOW!

■ Read the passage.
Fastest Car Window Opened by a Dog, September, 2004

Striker is a dog with a unique talent. He can roll down a car window with his paw. He does not do it by pushing a button. He does it the old-fashioned way. He **cranks** it down using a handle. Striker can do this very quickly. In fact, he is the Guinness World Records™ record-holder for dogs. He set this record in 2004 when he opened a car window in just 11.34 seconds.

Dogs are smart animals. They can learn many kinds of tricks. They can learn to sit or to jump through hoops. These are common tricks. Learning to roll down a car window is different. It is really a strange trick. Most owners would never think of teaching their dogs to do it. That is partly because most cars today have push-button windows. Only a few have handles to crank. Older cars are more likely to have windows with handles.

Francis Gadassi from Hungary happened to have a car with hand-cranked windows. He also had plenty of imagination. Gadassi trained Striker to use a front paw to roll down the car window. Striker had to turn the handle many times. Finally, the window was all the way down. Striker's record has held for several years. Do you know a dog that could break the record?

Name_____ Date_____

■ **Answer the questions.**

1. Circle *T* for true or *F* for false.

Striker taught himself to roll down a car window.   **T**   **F**

2. What kinds of tricks can many dogs do?

_____

_____

3. In this passage, **cranks** means:
   A. moves in a zigzag pattern
   B. turns with a handle
   C. makes something loose

4. Francis Gadassi is probably
   A. Striker's owner.
   B. a friend of Striker's owner.
   C. a race car driver.

5. In this passage, is it important that Striker's owner is a man? Why or why not?

_____

_____

■ **Choose one extension activity.**
   A. Think of a job that Striker could do using his special talent for turning a handle. Write a job description for that job.
   B. Imagine that Striker is coming to visit your school. Draw a poster to welcome him.

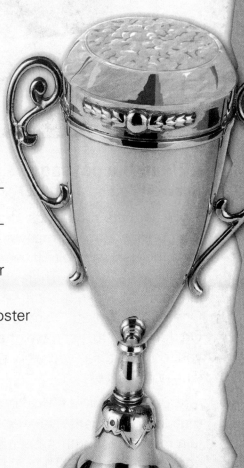

ALONG CAME A (VERY LARGE) SPIDER

■ Read the passage.
Heaviest Spider, July, 2007

There are thousands of different spiders in the world. They come in many sizes. The smallest is smaller than the head of a pin. It is so small that there is no record of its weight. Then, there is the Goliath bird-eating spider. It is the world's Heaviest Spider. One female Goliath, named Rosi, set the weight record. On July 27, 2007, she weighed 6.17 ounces (175 g). If you looked at her, you would see she is larger than a dinner plate.

Believe it or not, Rosi is a pet. She is owned by a man living in Austria. Austria is not Rosi's native home. In the wild, Goliath spiders live in the rain forests of South America. Their homes are dark holes in the dirt. They may build these homes themselves. They may also take over holes built by mice.

Like all spiders, the Goliath eats meat. It eats lizards and frogs. It also eats birds. That is why it is called a "bird-eating" spider. Some explorers first saw it **devouring** a hummingbird. Goliaths have sharp teeth called fangs. These fangs carry venom. But, a Goliath spider cannot kill you. Its bite may feel like a bee sting. However, its venom is harmless to humans.

DID YOU KNOW?
A rain forest is a thick forest that gets at least 100 inches (254 cm) of rain each year. Rain forests are hot, wet, and filled with life. They are home to millions of animals. Some animals, such as ants, are tiny. Other animals, such as gorillas, are very big.

Name_____ Date_____

■ Answer the questions.

1. Circle *T* for true or *F* for false.

   In the wild, Goliath spiders live in dark holes.   **T**   **F**

2. The Goliath spider eats
   - **A.** dirt.
   - **B.** bark.
   - **C.** meat.

3. What does the word **devouring** mean? What is something that might be seen devouring food?

   _____

   _____

4. The venom of a Goliath spider does not harm humans. What creatures do you think the venom might harm?

   _____

   _____

5. Do you think a Goliath spider would make a good monster in a scary movie? Why or why not?

   _____

   _____

   _____

■ Choose one extension activity.

   A. Find out more about various spiders in the rain forest. How many different kinds of spiders live in rain forests? What are two of the more interesting ones?

   B. Goliath spiders live in South America. Find South America on a map. What countries are on this continent? Where are the rain forests?

OPEN WIDE AND SAY "AHHHH"

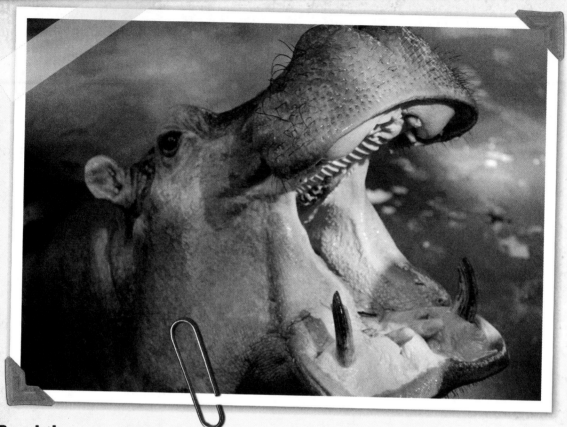

■ Read the passage.
Largest Mouth—Terrestrial Mammal

A lion has a big mouth. An elephant does too. But, the terrestrial (land) **mammal** with the biggest mouth is the hippopotamus. When an adult hippo opens his mouth, it can be 4 feet (1.2 m) wide. Inside that mouth are some very big teeth. Some are as long as your arm. The two biggest ones stick up from the bottom jaw. They can be 2.5 feet (46 cm) long!

It is not just a hippo's mouth that is big. These animals are big in other ways too. Male hippos can grow to more than 13 feet (4 m) in length. They can weigh up to 8,000 pounds (3,629 kg). Female hippos are smaller. They can weigh about 3,000 pounds (1,400 kg). That's about as heavy as a car.

What do hippos eat with their big mouths? It may surprise you to know that they are not meat eaters. Instead, they are **herbivores**. They eat grass that they find on riverbanks. Still, hippos can be dangerous to people. So, it is a good idea not to get close to them. If you want to look into a hippo's mouth, do it from far away!

Name_____ Date_____

■ Answer the questions.

1. Circle *T* for true or *F* for false.

   Male hippos are bigger than female hippos.   **T**   **F**

2. A hippo's biggest teeth are the ones that stick up from the _____ .

3. What are some characteristics of a **mammal**? What is your favorite mammal?

   _____

   _____

4. What are **herbivores**? Are you an herbivore?

   _____

   _____

5. What clues does the author give you about where hippos live?

   _____

   _____

■ Choose one statement. Then, explain why you agree or disagree.
   A. Zoos are good homes for hippos.
   B. A hippo would make a good pet.
   C. People should be allowed to go near hippos.

WHAT BIG EARS YOU HAVE!

■ Read the passage.
Longest Ears on a Rabbit, November 1, 2003

Many people think that rabbits make good pets. Rabbits are adorable. They have cute little noses. They have soft fur. They also have long ears. If you like really long ears, you might like English Lop rabbits. They have the Longest Ears on a Rabbit. In 2003, an English Lop rabbit set a new world record for ear length. The rabbit's name was Nipper's Geronimo. His ears were measured from the tip of one to the tip of the other. The total was 31.125 inches (79 cm). That is almost as long as a yardstick.

DID YOU KNOW?

Rabbits can make good pets. They enjoy playing with people and can be trained to use litter boxes. Some people keep them outside. Others keep them inside but take them out for walks on leashes. Rabbits are most active early in the day and late in the afternoon. They need plenty of water. A small rabbit drinks as much water as a 20-pound (9-kg) dog.

English Lop rabbits are not very active. They can become overweight if they eat too much. They love fresh hay, fresh fruit, and vegetables. These rabbits have **delicate** stomachs. Too many new foods at once could make them sick. They also need large **hutches**. They do not need the space to run. They need room for their ears to lie on the floor. Without space, they would step on their ears. For the English Lop rabbit, that could be a real danger.

Name_____ Date_____

■ Answer the questions.

1. English Lop rabbits have the longest _____ of any rabbit.

2. What are **hutches**? Would you need a hutch if you had a pet rabbit?

   _____

   _____

3. The word **delicate** is an adjective. In this passage, it describes a rabbit's stomach. What else could you describe as delicate?

   _____

   _____

4. Do you think that Nipper's Geronimo hears better than other English Lop rabbits? Why or why not?

   _____

   _____

■ Choose one extension activity.

A. Find a nursery rhyme or children's story about a rabbit. Learn about the history of this nursery rhyme or story. When and where was it written? Who is the author?

B. Research to learn more about wild rabbits. Where do wild rabbits live? How do they live?

ONE TRICKY FISH

■ Read the passage.

Fish with Largest Repertoire of Tricks, October 25, 2005

How smart are goldfish? Actually, they are smarter than you might think. Take, for example, a pet goldfish named Albert Einstein. In 2005, this goldfish set a new Guinness World Records™ record for doing more tricks than any other fish.

Albert Einstein the fish was named after a famous scientist. This fish was trained by Mr. Dean Pomerleau (USA) and his nine-year-old son, Kyle. They got the idea after Kyle won two goldfish at a school fair. Mr. Pomerleau saw that the fish **responded** to them when they came near the tank. Then, Mr. Pomerleau read some articles about how smart fish are. After that, he and his son decided to train one. "It's been a fun project for the two of us," said Mr. Pomerleau.

Often, animals are trained using a food reward. That is what Mr. Pomerleau and his son did. They gave Albert Einstein food whenever he did something right. In time, the fish understood: "Do this, get food." The fish learned six tricks. He learned to swim through hoops and tunnels. He learned to knock a soccer ball into a net. He even learned to wiggle like he was dancing. It takes a pretty smart fish to learn all of those tricks.

Name_____ Date_____

■ Answer the questions.

1. Circle *T* for true or *F* for false.

Kyle Pomerleau and his father had fun training Albert Einstein.　　**T**　　**F**

2. Albert Einstein the fish is named after a famous _____ .

3. Albert Einstein does tricks to
   A. make the Pomerleaus happy.
   B. show how smart he is.
   C. get a food reward.

4. What does **responded** mean?

_____

_____

5. What is one trick that you would like to teach Albert Einstein?

_____

_____

6. Do you think Albert Einstein's soccer ball was the same kind that you would use in a soccer game? Why or why not?

_____

_____

■ Choose one extension activity.

A. Imagine that you are the owner of Albert Einstein the fish. Write a journal entry telling how it feels to own the world's trickiest fish.

B. Write an advertisement for a show about Albert Einstein the fish. Share your advertisement with your classmates.

A TOY-SIZED HORSE

■ Read the passage.
Smallest Living Horse, July 7, 2006

What would you name the smallest horse in the world? Kay and Paul Goessling (USA) faced this question. In 2001, a tiny horse was born on their farm. She weighed 8 1/2 pounds (3.9 kg). That is about the size of a human baby. When this horse **matured**, she was only 17 1/2 inches (44.5 cm) tall. In 2006, the horse was named the Smallest Living Horse. In fact, she is the smallest horse on record. What name fits such a tiny horse? The Goesslings chose the name Thumbelina.

The Goesslings knew that Thumbelina would be small. Her parents were less than 3 feet (1 m) tall. Other horses stand 5 feet (1.5 m) or more. Still, she is much smaller than anyone expected. She is about half the size of her parents.

Thumbelina fits in with all of the animals on the farm. The dogs even let her sleep in their doghouse. Thumbelina helps sick children. She lets them pet her and hug her. With millions of fans around the world, this little horse has turned out to be a big hit.

DID YOU KNOW?
Miniature horses are sometimes used as guide animals for people who are blind. Like guide dogs, these horses are calm, careful, and smart. They have excellent eyesight and memory. In some ways, they are better than guide dogs. They live much longer than guide dogs. They are also great for people who are allergic to dogs.

■ Answer the questions.

1. Circle *T* for true or *F* for false.

   The Goesslings expected Thumbelina to be a big horse.   **T**   **F**

2. Thumbelina likes to sleep in the
   A. Goesslings' house.
   B. doghouse.
   C. stable.

3. What does **matured** mean? Do all living things mature the same way?

   _____

   _____

4. Based on this passage, what would you guess a normal-sized horse weighs at birth?
   A. about 2 pounds (0.9 kg)
   B. about 9 pounds (4.1 kg)
   C. about 100 pounds (45 kg)

5. Name three ways that Thumbelina is special.

   _____

   _____

6. Do you think that sick children would like Thumbelina as much if she were a normal-sized horse? Explain your answer.

   _____

   _____

■ Choose one statement. Then, explain why you agree or disagree.

A. Horse owners should not be allowed to bring their horses to public parks.
B. Miniature horses make better pets than normal-sized horses.

NOW THAT'S AN EGG!

■ Read the passage.

Largest Egg from a Living Bird, May 17, 2008

This record-breaking egg is from a living bird. Dinosaurs laid larger eggs. But, dinosaurs are **extinct**, so they don't count. Among living birds, the ostrich is the clear winner. An average ostrich egg weighs about 3.3 pounds (1.5 kg). That is about the size of 24 chicken eggs. This egg was laid in Sweden in 2008. It weighed 5 pounds 11 ounces (2.589 kg).

The owners of the ostrich farm, Gunnar and Kerstin Sahlin (Sweden), were surprised by the size of this egg. Their ostriches have laid giant eggs before. Twice in the past, one of their ostrich eggs has held the world record. Still, they were not expecting to win in 2008. As soon as the Sahlins saw the egg, they knew that it was special. They rushed it to the post office. There, it was weighed. The Sahlins were thrilled by the size. Someone asked what they might do with the egg. "We are thinking about baking a giant cake," answered Kerstin Sahlin.

DID YOU KNOW?

An ostrich egg has a tough shell. It has to be pretty tough. A 300-pound (136-kg) bird sits on it. The hard shell makes it perfect for artists to decorate. First, the egg is drained. This is done by drilling a hole in the bottom. Then, the shell is washed and wiped clean. Ostrich shells are shipped to egg artists around the world.

22

Name_____ Date_____

■ Answer the questions.

1. The Sahlins had their egg weighed at the _____ .

2. What does **extinct** mean? How do you feel when you learn about an animal becoming extinct?

   _____

   _____

3. What experiences have the Sahlins had with record-breaking ostrich eggs?

   _____

   _____

4. Would you rather own the largest egg in the world or the smallest egg in the world? Explain your answer.

   _____

   _____

5. Why do you think that ostrich eggs are so much bigger than chicken eggs?

   _____

   _____

■ Choose one extension activity.

A. Become an egg artist. Use a clean, drained eggshell or hard-boiled egg and decorate your own egg. Create a display of all of the decorated eggs that you and your classmates make.

B. Write a "For Sale" ad for the world's Largest Egg from a Living Bird. Think about how to attract a customer. What will you say about the egg? What will your selling price be?

GIANT TORTOISE

■ Read the passage.
Largest Tortoise

The Galápagos Islands are located off the coast of South America. They are named for their giant tortoises. *Galápago* is a Spanish word meaning *saddle*. A Galápagos tortoise shell looks a little like a saddle. This **species** of tortoise is the largest in the world. The very largest one was named Goliath. He weighed 920 pounds (417 kg). That is about half the weight of a small car. He was 53 inches (135.8 cm) long and 27 inches (68.5 cm) tall.

Galápagos tortoises need room to graze. They have been called "eating machines." They eat lots of grass, vines, and fruit. But, they do not need to eat very often. They can store food and water for a long time. In fact, they can live for months without any food or water. These tortoises live a long time. The oldest one on record lived 152 years. Sadly, many have not lived to old age. They have been hunted by humans. There were once over 250,000. Now there are only 15,000 of these **endangered** tortoises.

DID YOU KNOW?
Galápagos tortoises may be big, but they are not fast. They move so slowly that it would take a tortoise more than six hours to cover 1 mile (1.6 km). The average person could walk that distance in about 20 minutes.

Name_____ Date_____

■ Answer the questions.

1. Galápagos tortoises eat _____ .

2. Circle *T* for true or *F* for false.

   Galápagos tortoises are often called fighting machines.   **T**   **F**

3. In this passage, the word **endangered** means:
   - **A.** in danger of dying out
   - **B.** causing danger to others
   - **C.** unaware of the dangers around it

4. How have humans caused problems for the Galápagos tortoise?

   _____

   _____

5. Do you think that a Galápagos tortoise would be happy in a city? Why or why not?

   _____

   _____

6. Would you like to live to be 152 years old? Why or why not?

   _____

   _____

■ Choose one extension activity.

A. The Galápagos tortoise is an endangered **species**. What is a species? Find another endangered species and learn about it.

B. Locate the Galápagos Islands on a map. Find out more about these islands, such as how many islands there are, what country they belong to, and how far they are from the mainland of that country.

REACHING FOR THE SKY

■ Read the passage.
Tallest Mammal

An adult giraffe is about 18 feet (5.5 m) tall. That makes it the Tallest Mammal in the world. Among giraffes, the Guinness World Records™ record-holder is a male named George. Born in the wild in Kenya, George stood 19 feet (5.8 m) tall. In 1959, he was brought to a zoo in England. He lived there until he died in 1969.

In a zoo, height may not matter. In the wild, though, being tall is a good thing. It allows giraffes to spot a predator a long way off. This gives them time to run. A giraffe warns the other members of the herd with a snort. Then, the entire herd dashes away.

A giraffe's height is good for another reason too. Giraffes are **vegetarians**. They do not prey on other animals. Instead, giraffes eat tree leaves. Their height allows them to reach the tender leaves on high branches. Their tongues also help with this. A giraffe's tongue is up to 2 feet (61 cm) long. It is perfect for grabbing and holding leaves. That helps a giraffe eat up to 100 pounds (45 kg) of leaves a day.

But, a giraffe's height can be a bad thing. Giraffes' long legs make them slow to stand up when they are on the ground. This could be a problem if a predator is attacking. So, giraffes do not usually lie down. They even sleep on their feet. Giraffes are truly amazing animals. There is no other animal like them.

■ Answer the questions.

1. The tallest giraffe ever measured was named
    A. George.
    B. Chester.
    C. Kenya.

2. Circle *T* for true or *F* for false.

    Giraffes hardly ever lie down.   **T   F**

3. **Vegetarians** are creatures that do not eat _____.

4. Giraffes snort to alert each other to danger. What sounds do humans use to warn of danger?

    _____

    _____

5. A giraffe's height is helpful in some ways but not in others. How can being tall help a human? In what way might it be a problem?

    _____

    _____

■ Choose one extension activity.

A. Write three questions that you have about giraffes. Compare your questions to those of your classmates.

B. Write a list of six animals that probably live in the wild in Kenya. Then, see how many of your guesses are correct.

BABY BOOM

■ **Read the passage.**

Most Dolphins Born in a Year in a Single Facility, December 4, 2008

The Delphinus Xcaret aquarium in Mexico is home to bottlenose dolphins. In 2008, this aquarium set a new world record. In that one year, female dolphins gave birth to 11 babies. Never before had that many dolphins been born in one place. Better yet, they all lived. In aquariums, dolphin survival rate is about 60 percent, or a little more than half. Even fewer dolphins survive in the ocean. So, the 100 percent rate was a happy surprise. The dolphins deserve much of the credit. Older females helped the new mothers. Humans helped too. They offered the best possible care.

Of course, just about everyone loves dolphins. And, why not? Dolphins do amazing tricks. They understand human commands. They also "talk" to each other. They do this by making sounds. These include a kind of whistle. Dolphins also use their bodies to **communicate**. One way is by hitting their flippers on the surface of the water. Dolphins even jump out of the water and land with a big splash. That sends a message too.

Dolphins are very active. Yet, they need their sleep. As they sleep, they may swim very slowly, or they may rest on the bottom. Every now and then, they come to the surface. They take a quick breath of air. Then, they go underwater again. Dolphins sleep this way for about eight hours each day.

Name_____ Date_____

■ Answer the questions.

1. The new mother dolphins were helped by

    A. older female dolphins.

    B. humans.

    C. older female dolphins and humans.

2. Circle *T* for true or *F* for false.

    Baby dolphins cannot survive in the wild.   **T**   **F**

3. In this passage, the word **communicate** means _____ .
Give an example of how you communicate.

_____

_____

4. How do dolphins communicate with each other?

_____

_____

5. Dolphins do not use words to communicate. How can humans communicate without words?

_____

_____

6. Dolphins swim while they are asleep. What can the human body do while sleeping?

_____

_____

■ Choose one extension activity.

A. Make up your own sign language for "yes" and "no." Compare your signs with those made by classmates.

B. Make a list of five names that you think would be good names for a baby dolphin. Explain why you chose these names. Compare your list with your classmates' lists. Are any of the names the same?

TOO BIG FOR A BOWL

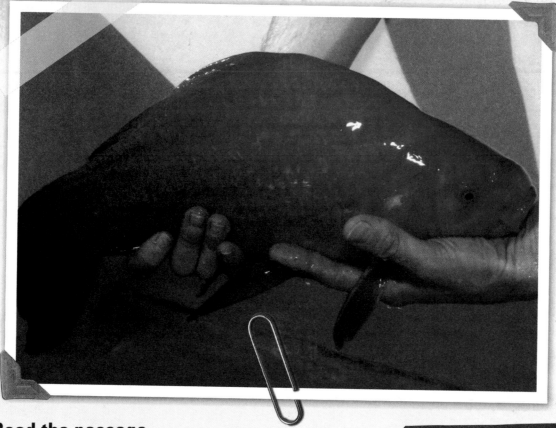

■ Read the passage.
Longest Goldfish, March 24, 2003

How long is a goldfish? The ones you might see in a fish tank may be just 1 or 2 inches (2.5 to 5 cm) long. If you buy one, you might put it in a goldfish bowl. These bowls are not very big. The size of the bowl does not matter because the goldfish itself is not big. Now, imagine a giant goldfish. The world's Longest Goldfish measured is 18.7 inches (47.4 cm) long from snout to tail fin. That is about as long as a newborn baby. This Guinness World Records™ record-breaking goldfish belongs to Joris Gijsbers of the Netherlands.

All goldfish start out small. They grow bigger as they get older. How much they grow depends on several things. It depends on how much food they get. It also depends on the size of their tanks. A goldfish kept in a bowl or small tank will never grow very large. That is one reason why some people **establish** goldfish ponds. These are set up outdoors. Goldfish ponds may have 300 gallons (1,136 L) of water or more. That gives the goldfish much more room to move around. Goldfish in ponds may grow to be about 10 inches (25.4 cm) long. Still, that is much smaller than Gijsbers's fish. Other fish owners may dream of owning the longest goldfish. In Joris Gijsbers's case, that dream came true.

DID YOU KNOW?
Many goldfish are gold. However, they can be other colors. They can be yellow, silver, or red. They can even be black. Most goldfish might live for four years or so. In the best conditions, a goldfish might live for more than 20 years.

Name_____ Date_____

■ Answer the questions.

1. Circle *T* for true or *F* for false.

Most goldfish can be kept in small bowls.   **T**   **F**

2. Name two things that can affect a goldfish's size.

_____

_____

3. In this passage, the word **establish** means _____.

4. People may set up goldfish ponds to grow bigger goldfish. Can you think of other reasons why someone might set up a goldfish pond?

_____

_____

5. Would you rather have a big goldfish or a small goldfish for a pet? Explain your answer.

_____

_____

■ Choose one extension activity.

A. A goldfish has a snout and a tail fin. Research to learn the other body parts of a goldfish.

B. How and where did goldfish first appear in history? Have goldfish changed over time? Write a short report on your findings.

A BEETLE NAMED GOLIATH

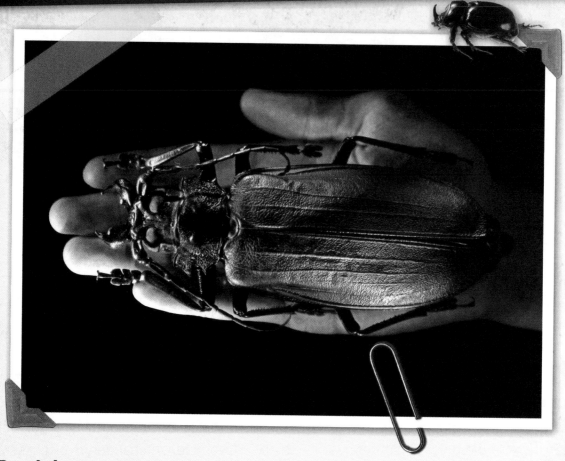

■ Read the passage.
Largest Species of Beetle

Some beetles may be longer. Other beetles may be wider. For weight, however, the champion is the Goliath beetle. In fact, Goliath beetles are the heaviest of all insects. These beetles live on the continent of Africa. A fully-grown Goliath beetle can be 4.5 inches (11.43 cm) long. It can weigh up to 3.5 ounces (100 g).

Goliath beetles are amazing creatures. They help clean up the earth. They do this by eating dead leaves and other waste matter. The Goliath and its fellow beetles have been doing this sort of recycling for about 300 million years. Human beings got the idea just a little while ago! So, the next time you see a beetle, think of it as a friend, not an insect.

Many other creatures have come and gone. So, how have beetles survived so long? One reason is that beetles can **adapt** to changes in the world. They know how to deal with heat or cold. They do not seem to mind if it is wet or dry. Beetles have a hard, thin shell over their wings. This protects their wings. Some beetles trap water inside this shell. This helps them live in deserts. Other beetles use their shells to trap air. These beetles can live underwater. If humans ever disappear from the earth, it is a good bet that beetles will be there to say good-bye.

Name_____ Date_____

■ Answer the questions.

1. The Goliath beetle is found on the continent of _____ .

2. Circle *T* for true or *F* for false.

   Beetles have been around for about 300 million years.   **T**   **F**

3. In this passage, the word **adapt** means:
   - **A.** change to fit new conditions
   - **B.** become the biggest and strongest
   - **C.** be less frightened

4. Why does the author say that you should think of a beetle as your friend?

   _____

   _____

5. Do you think that beetles would have a harder time surviving if they did not have hard shells over their wings? Why or why not?

   _____

   _____

■ Choose one statement. Then, explain why you agree or disagree.
   - **A.** Recycling is a waste of time.
   - **B.** Human beings are not very good at adapting to changes on Earth.

A DOG AND A CAN

■ Read the passage.

Fastest 100 Meters with a Can Balanced on Head—Dog, September 3, 2008

In 2008, Sweet Pea set a new Guinness World Records™ record. She walked 100 meters (328 feet) while balancing a can on her head. That is a little more than the length of a football field. She did not drop the can even once. It took her 2 minutes, 55 seconds. Sweet Pea is a mixed breed dog. She is half collie and half shepherd.

Sweet Pea is a special dog. She also holds the record for Most Jumps with a Jump Rope in One Minute. In 2007, Sweet Pea became a TV star in Germany. She appeared on a game show. More than 13 million people watched her. They were amazed. They saw her walk up and down stairs with a glass of water on her head. Sweet Pea did not spill a drop. Newspapers hailed her as a "super dog." Other dog owners wondered if they could teach their dogs such tricks.

The answer is probably no. Collies are more trainable than most other dog breeds, so it is easier for them to learn tricks. Also, many hours of training are needed. Owner Alex Rothacker (USA) is a professional dog handler. He spent five years training Sweet Pea. He worked with her for two or three hours nearly every day. There are not many dog owners with that kind of **dedication**.

Name_____ Date_____

■ Answer the questions.

1. Circle *T* for true or *F* for false.

Sweet Pea is half collie and half shepherd.   **T**   **F**

2. Sweet Pea holds the record for the Fastest 100 Meters with a Can Balanced on Head—Dog. What other record does Sweet Pea hold?

_____

_____

3. What does **dedication** mean? What is something that you have shown dedication to?

_____

_____

4. Why is Sweet Pea famous in Germany?

_____

_____

5. The passage suggests that
- **A.** it took a lot of work for Sweet Pea to learn these tricks.
- **B.** Sweet Pea would be able to teach these tricks to other dogs.
- **C.** newspapers reported things about Sweet Pea that were not true.

■ Choose one extension activity.

A. Write a TV commercial that will encourage viewers to watch Sweet Pea on the game show.

B. Find five friends who own dogs. Ask them what tricks, if any, their dogs can do. Create a chart showing your findings.

REVIEW: AMAZING ANIMALS

■ **Find the words hidden in the puzzle. The words may be found across or down.**

adapt	devouring	matured
cranks	establish	responded
communicate	extinct	species
dedication	hutch	vegetarian
delicate	mammal	

v	a	m	m	e	d	e	v	o	u	r	i	n	g	s
e	g	a	x	l	e	s	p	e	x	o	c	a	c	d
g	h	p	i	p	d	e	l	i	c	a	t	e	y	v
e	u	d	q	g	i	t	r	n	i	m	n	e	n	w
t	r	a	r	n	c	o	x	o	p	i	i	x	a	g
a	e	d	e	m	a	t	u	r	e	d	o	t	d	u
r	g	a	e	a	t	d	v	e	d	a	r	i	t	u
i	e	p	v	a	i	n	c	o	m	m	u	n	d	s
a	m	t	b	n	o	a	p	r	a	r	h	c	r	p
n	r	c	r	a	n	k	s	e	m	a	a	t	a	e
i	a	e	d	e	v	o	a	m	m	m	v	o	x	c
e	s	t	a	b	l	i	s	h	a	a	s	t	p	i
n	t	e	h	u	t	c	h	i	l	p	h	v	e	e
d	a	c	o	m	m	u	n	i	c	a	t	e	s	s
e	c	a	v	e	g	r	e	s	p	o	n	d	e	d

Name_____ Date_____

REVIEW: AMAZING ANIMALS

■ **Write the correct word in each blank to complete the passage.**

dog	hippo
dolphin	horses
giraffe	ostrich
goldfish	tortoise

The animal world is filled with amazing creatures. There is the _____
(1)

that lays five-pound (2.25 kg) eggs. A _____ can live for months without food
(2)

or water. And, the _____ has teeth as long as your arm!
(3)

Many animals have their own forms of communication. For example, a

_____ talks using whistles. A _____ uses a snort to
(4)   (5)

warn of danger. Some animals are very good at learning commands given by humans. That

is true of Albert Einstein. A human taught this _____ to knock a soccer ball
(6)

into a net! Another example is Sweet Pea. This _____ learned to walk
(7)

100 meters (328 feet) with a can balanced on her head. Some animals even learn to help

humans. That is true of miniature _____ . They can be trained to be guide
(8)

animals for blind people.

THAT'S A LOT OF HAIR!

■ Read the passage.
Longest Hair (Female), May 8, 2004

Xie Qiuping (China) holds the record for the longest hair of any woman in the world. Many women like to wear their hair long. Still, they usually have it trimmed every couple of months. That is not the case with Xie Qiuping. She did not cut her hair for more than 35 years!

Xie Qiuping started growing her hair long in 1973. She was 13 years old at the time. By May 8, 2004, her hair had grown very long. It was long enough to set a Guinness World Records™ record. It measured 18 feet 5.54 inches (5.627 m). That is more than three times as long as her entire body.

It is not easy to grow hair this long. Hair grows well only when you have a healthy body and a healthy **diet.** Long hair also requires a lot of care. Washing it takes time. Brushing it also takes time. Still, Xie Qiuping insists that her long hair is not a burden. "It's no trouble at all," she says.

Xie Qiuping sometimes wears her hair tied up. Other times she lets it all down. When she wears her hair loose, she needs an assistant to hold it so that it does not drag on the ground. People love to see her long hair. Sometimes, she displays it on stage or at weddings. Her hair helps make her famous wherever she goes.

DID YOU KNOW?
If you are like most people, you have over 100,000 hairs on your head. The hair on your head grows at about the same speed. For most people, that is about 0.5 inches (1.27 cm) per month. That means it takes a year for your hair to grow 6 inches (15.24 cm)!

■ Answer the questions.

1. Xie Qiuping stopped having her hair cut when she was _____ years old.

2. Xie Qiuping says that having such long hair is

    A. a good way to make money.

    B. quite a burden.

    C. no trouble at all.

3. In this passage, the word **diet** means _____ .
In what ways is your diet healthy?

_____

_____

4. Imagine that you have hair as long as Xie Qiuping's. When might it get in your way?

_____

_____

■ Choose one extension activity.

A. Xie Qiuping's hair measured close to 20 feet (6.1 m). Research other things that might be 20 feet long or might grow to be 20 feet tall.

B. Xie Qiuping is from China. Find China on a map. Then, gather three facts about China, such as its mountains or rivers.

A DIFFERENT KIND OF MONSTER

■ Read the passage.
Largest Monster Truck, 1986

People call it *Bigfoot 5*. Is it a movie monster? No, it is the Largest Monster Truck in the world. It weighs 38,000 pounds (17,236 kg). That is more than two elephants put together! *Bigfoot 5* is almost as tall as a giraffe. It is 15 feet 6 inches (4.7 m) tall. It has tires that are 10 feet (3 m) tall.

Bigfoot 5 was built by Bob and Marilyn Chandler (USA). They have built more than 12 monster trucks. A monster truck is not used for trucking. It is not used to carry logs or steel. Instead, monster trucks are used to entertain fans. They are just for fun.

Monster trucks compete against each other. They race on a track filled with **obstacles**. An obstacle might be a small plane or an old school bus. Monster trucks do not drive around these things. They run over them! That is the fun part. Monster trucks crush obstacles under their huge tires. Several of these trucks tour the country. People love seeing what these giant trucks can do.

DID YOU KNOW?
Drivers get into monster trucks by climbing up through a **hatch** in the floor. If there is no hatch, they grab the door handle and pull themselves up. Monster truck drivers wear special suits and gloves that do not burn easily. They also wear special seat belts, helmets, and neck collars to protect themselves when they hit something.

Name_____ Date_____

■ **Answer the questions.**

1. How big are *Bigfoot 5*'s tires?

_____

2. What is the best meaning for the word **obstacles**?
   A. items that do not belong
   B. things that block a path
   C. dangerous problems

3. Regular trucks carry products such as steel and logs. Why don't monster trucks carry such things?

   _____

   _____

4. Imagine that you have been asked to give *Bigfoot 5* a new name. What name would you choose and why?

   _____

   _____

5. Would you like to ride in a monster truck? Why or why not?

   _____

   _____

6. What other vehicles or buildings might have a **hatch**?

   _____

   _____

■ **Choose one extension activity.**
   A. Research to learn about the history of monster trucks.
   B. Gather information about today's monster trucks, such as how fast they go and how much they cost.

CALLING ALL BIRDS

■ Read the passage.
Largest Bird Feeder (Volume), February 26, 2009

In 2009, a huge bird feeder was built in the United Kingdom. It was so big that it set a new Guinness World Records™ record. The feeder was 11 feet 5 inches (3.5 m) tall. That is taller than a basketball hoop. It held 213 pounds 13 ounces (97 kg) of bird food. The bird feeder had sunflower seeds and wheat in it. There were also other seeds that birds love.

Why build such a giant bird feeder? The people who did were trying to gain attention. They wanted to spread the word about a problem. The problem is that farmland birds in the United Kingdom are dying off. This includes birds such as sparrows. There are only half as many farmland birds now as there were in the 1970s. One reason for this is that bird **habitats** are disappearing. There was once plenty of open land for these birds. Now, humans are using more and more of it. This makes it harder for birds to survive. They cannot find food during the winter or in early spring.

One way to solve this problem is to plant more crops that wild birds eat. Another solution is to put up more bird feeders. This is where the giant bird feeder comes in. It is so big that it catches people's attention. That may start people talking about the problem. And, talking about the problem might be the first step toward solving it.

Name_____ Date_____

■ Answer the questions.

1. What is happening to the farmland birds of the United Kingdom?

_____

_____

2. According to this passage, farmland birds eat
    A. nuts and berries.
    B. various seeds.
    C. many kinds of bugs.

3. What are **habitats**? What animal habitats exist near your home?

_____

_____

4. Do you think that the United Kingdom is the only place where animals are losing their habitats? Explain your answer.

_____

_____

5. Judging from this passage, how does human activity affect animals?

_____

_____

■ Choose one extension activity.

A. Working in small groups, design and build a bird feeder. As you do this, try to reuse and recycle products from around your home or school. Compare your bird feeder with those made by other groups in your class.

B. Write a speech explaining why it is important to protect the habitats of birds in your area. Try to make your speech two to three minutes long.

STRETCHY SKIN

■ Read the passage.
Stretchiest Skin, October 29, 1999

Garry Turner (United Kingdom) has stretchy skin. In fact, he has the Stretchiest Skin on record. In 1999, he extended the skin on his stomach 6.22 inches (15.8 cm). Just hold a ballpoint pen straight out from your stomach. That is about how far out Turner can pull his skin.

There is a reason why Turner's skin is so stretchy. He has a rare condition. It is called Ehlers-Danlos syndrome, or EDS. In most human bodies, cells are held together by a protein. It is called collagen. You can think of it as glue for your body. People with EDS have **faulty** "glue." Their collagen does not **bind** cells tightly to each other. That makes their skin very, very loose. Turner says his skin is like a badly woven basket. It stretches very easily.

Do not feel sorry for Garry Turner. He doesn't. He has learned to live with EDS. Actually, he makes his living with it. He tours with a circus. People are amazed by his loose skin. Turner says that he loves being on stage. He loves making people smile. "I don't want people to feel any sorrow for me in any kind of way," he says.

DID YOU KNOW?
EDS is a fairly rare condition. It strikes about one person in 5,000. It does not affect just the skin. It also affects a person's joints. The joints may be so loose that it hurts just to walk. Some people have mild cases of EDS. Garry Turner has an unusually severe case.

Name_____ Date_____

1. Garry Turner set the record by stretching the skin on his
   A. stomach.
   B. arm.
   C. neck.

2. Circle *T* for true or *F* for false.

   If something is **faulty**, it does not work correctly.   **T**   **F**

3. What do you think would happen if a person had no collagen at all?

   _____

   _____

4. What does **bind** mean? Name two items that people use to bind things to each other.

   _____

   _____

5. How do you think that Garry Turner feels about having EDS?

   _____

   _____

■ **Choose one extension activity.**

A. Look around your home. List five things that stretch. Compare your list to your classmates. What is the stretchy thing that your class listed most often?

B. Draw a picture showing what you think you would look like with stretchy skin.

© Carson-Dellosa   45

AN EYE FOR A RECORD

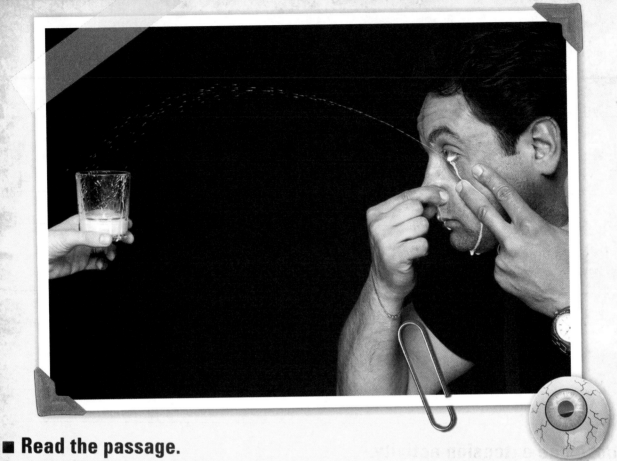

■ Read the passage.
Farthest Milk Squirting Distance, September 1, 2004

Some Guinness World Records™ records attract a lot of **competition**. For example, many people try to be the fastest or strongest. Other records are just weird. What Ilker Yilmaz (Turkey) does is one of the weird ones. He can squirt milk out of his eye! In 2004, he squirted milk from his left eye a record distance of 9 feet 2 inches (279.5 cm).

How does this man from Turkey do it? First, he pours some milk into his hand. He snorts it up his nose. Then, he pulls back his left eyelid. Somehow, he is able to shoot the milk out of his eye. This is truly a strange trick. But, Yilmaz is proud for getting his country into the *Guinness World Records* book. Only a few people can do what he does. You need to be born with a link between your nose and your eye.

Yilmaz was not the first to squirt milk from his eye. He broke an old record. It was set by a man from Canada. For years, Yilmaz knew that he had this ability. He discovered it as a boy, while he was swimming. He noticed water would squirt out of his eye. Years passed. Then, one day he saw a man on TV. The man was trying to set a record for squirting liquid out of his eye. Yilmaz thought, "Maybe, I could do that too." Three years later, Ilker Yilmaz set a new world record.

Name_____ Date_____

■ Answer the questions.

1. The young Yilmaz first noticed his ability while he was _____.

2. Squirting milk out of the eye is
   A. a rare talent.
   B. very dangerous.
   C. easier for men than women.

3. What does **competition** mean? What is one event in your school or town that draws a lot of competition?

   _____

   _____

4. Why do you think Yilmaz chooses to squirt milk instead of something like lemon juice or salt water?

   _____

   _____

■ Choose one statement. Then, explain why you agree or disagree.

A. Ilker Yilmaz's milk-squirting ability is weird and strange.
B. People should not be allowed to squirt milk from their eyes on TV.

A HOUSE MADE OF ICE

■ Read the passage.

Largest Dome Igloo, February 17, 2008

Do you live where there is ice in the winter? If so, you might have fun sliding on it. But, for some people, ice has an important purpose. It is used to build igloos. Igloos are dome-shaped houses. The Largest Dome Igloo ever recorded was built in Canada. It measured 25 feet 9 inches (7.85 m) across. That is almost wide enough to fit two cars end to end. It was 13 feet 8 inches (4.17 m) high.

This igloo was built during a competition between different teams. The winning team had 70 volunteers. They spent 50 hours and used 2,000 blocks of ice. They had to build the igloo from the ground up. It could not be carved out of a larger pile of snow and ice.

The hard-working team did a lot of planning. Their finished igloo was safe and solid. It could hold more than 200 people at the same time. It lasted 59 days. Finally, warm April weather caused it to **collapse**. However, the record still stands!

DID YOU KNOW?

The word *igloo* means *house*. The Inuit invented the igloo centuries ago. They had to be creative. They did not have wood or bricks for building homes. They had to use what was handy—snow! Inuit hunters often went on long trips that lasted for many days. An igloo made from snow gave them quick protection at night from the cold.

Name_____ Date_____

■ Answer the questions.

1. Circle *T* for true or *F* for false.

The finished igloo could hold more than 200 people at once.   **T   F**

2. The competition was to see who could build the _____ igloo.

3. In this passage, the word **collapse** means:

    A. fall down

    B. freeze

    C. full of holes

4. Do you think one person working alone could have built this igloo? Why or why not?

_____

_____

5. Why is Canada a better place to build igloos than Mexico?

_____

_____

■ Choose one extension activity.

    A. Use sugar cubes and glue to construct your own mini-igloo. Is it easy to do? How big can you make it?

    B. Imagine you are the leader of a team that is trying to build the biggest igloo ever. Write a list of rules for your team to follow. Explain why each rule is important for your team's success.

AFRICA'S BIG SNAIL

■ Read the passage.
Largest Snail, December 1978

Snails come in many varieties. The largest ones are from Africa. A giant tiger snail was the biggest ever recorded. It was found in Sierra Leone. It weighed 2 pounds (900 g), which is more than two cans of soup. Its shell measured 10.75 inches (27.3 cm). That is almost as long as a ruler. A snail this large deserves a name. Its owners called it Gee Geronimo.

Many people do not like snails. They find them gross and slimy. Snails produce slime, or mucus, to help them move. They travel by sliding along small rivers of their slime. Snail slime is sticky. It helps snails stick to all kinds of surfaces. Snails need water to make slime. That is why they do not like hot, dry conditions.

Some people love to have snails as pets. A fish tank can be a good home for a snail. But, snails reproduce quickly. One snail may have 10 babies at once! Most pet snails are small, but giant African snails are huge. The United States does not allow them as pets. They can be a **threat** to crops. So, if you live in the U.S. and want a pet snail, please make it a small one.

DID YOU KNOW?
Snail slime is a beauty product. It is used in some skin creams. It is supposed to keep your skin silky smooth. Some people want nothing to do with slimy skin cream. However, others say that it works great. They love to buy skin cream that contains snail slime.

Name_____ Date_____

■ Answer the questions.

1. Circle *T* for true or *F* for false.

   The world's largest snails are found in South America.   **T**   **F**

2. How do snails use the slime that they produce?

   _____

   _____

3. A synonym is a word that has the same meaning as another word. What is a synonym
   for **threat**?

   _____

4. The author writes that snails "travel by sliding along small rivers of their slime." What might
   be a better word for "rivers"?
   - **A.** oceans
   - **B.** trails
   - **C.** openings

5. If you owned the largest snail in the world, what would you name it and why?

   _____

   _____

■ Choose one extension activity.
   - **A.** Do you think snails are cool or gross? Write a poem that expresses your feelings
     about snails.
   - **B.** Draw a funny cartoon showing a snail leaving a trail of slime over some object or
     room in your home or classroom. Be sure to give your cartoon a title.

GREAT BALL OF FUN

■ Read the passage.
Largest Ball of Plastic Wrap, June 14, 2007

Jake Lonsway (USA) is one of the youngest Guinness World Records™ record-holders. He was just seven years old when he set his record. It is for the Largest Ball of Plastic Wrap. It took Lonsway eight months to create the ball. On June 14, 2007, he had it officially weighed. The ball weighed 281 pounds 8 ounces (127.7 kg). It measured 138 inches (351 cm) in **circumference**. That is about the size of a large exercise ball.

Lonsway had wanted to break some kind of record. His parents had looked at the *Guinness World Records Book*. They wanted to find a record that Lonsway could try to beat. They found the record for plastic wrap. At that time, the record was 250 pounds (113 kg). Soon after that, Lonsway's mother brought home a ball of plastic wrap the size of a softball. The rest is history.

Lonsway kept adding more plastic wrap. His mother brought home leftover wrap from her job. Friends and neighbors also pitched in with more wrap. The ball grew and grew. It took up a lot of space in the house. So, Lonsway moved it to the garage. After setting the record, the ball was moved once more. Today, it is in a children's museum in Michigan.

Name_____ Date_____

■ Answer the questions.

1. Who helped Lonsway collect plastic wrap for his ball?

_____

_____

2. Over time, Lonsway's ball of plastic wrap was kept in three places: a museum, a house, and a garage. Rearrange this list by writing in order where it was kept first, where it was kept second, and where it is now.

_____

_____

3. What is **circumference**? Name two things that have a circumference.

_____

_____

4. Do you use plastic wrap? If so, what do you use it for? What do you do with it when you are finished?

_____

_____

5. Why do you think the ball of plastic wrap went to a children's museum instead of an adult's museum?

_____

_____

■ Choose one extension activity.

A. Working in a small group, collect some common school or household supplies, such as rubber bands, masking tape, or aluminum foil. Use your supplies to make a ball. Compare your group's result with the results of other groups.

B. Create a work of art using sturdy paper, paint, and plastic wrap. Put blobs of paint on the paper. Then, while the paint is still wet, cover the blobs with a piece of plastic wrap. Crinkle the plastic wrap to form patterns and swirls in the paint. Let it dry. Then, remove the wrap and admire your creation!

53

THE TALLEST MAN IN THE WORLD

■ Read the passage.
**Tallest Living Man,
February 11, 2009**

Sultan Kosen from Turkey was a normal-sized 10-year-old farm boy. There was nothing about him that was out of the ordinary. Then, suddenly, all of that changed. He had a huge growth spurt. By the time Kosen was 12, he was the tallest boy in his school. As an adult, Kosen grew to become the world's Tallest Living Man. He reached 8 feet 1 inch (246.5 cm). If he stood flatfooted under a basketball hoop, he could easily touch the rim.

Why did Kosen grow so much? The reason is that he had a clump of cells, called a tumor, behind his eyes. The tumor pressed on his growth **gland**. As a result, Kosen kept growing. The doctors finally removed the tumor. But, by then, he was more than 8 feet (243.84 cm) tall.

Kosen has weak knees. This condition was caused by Kosen growing too fast. The joints did not form properly. Today, he must use walking sticks to help him get around. Still, Kosen is proud of his height. It has made him famous. After setting the world record, he said, "I was so proud for my family and for my country." Kosen also has a great sense of humor. He once was asked, "Are you taller than your father?" Kosen just smiled and said, "I'm taller than everyone's father!"

DID YOU KNOW?
You are taller in the morning than you are at night. During the night, you usually lie down. During the day, you are mostly upright. When you are upright, gravity pulls you down. So, as the day goes on, gravity shrinks your body just a little.

Name_____ Date_____

■ Answer the questions.

1. Circle *T* for true or *F* for false.

At age 10, Kosen was the tallest boy in his school. **T**   **F**

2. Kosen uses _____ to help him walk.

3. In this passage, the word **gland** means:
   A. an organ in the body that performs a certain function
   B. a disease that causes young children to grow rapidly
   C. an operation that can correct a problem in the body

4. Do you think Kosen's life would have been different if doctors had removed the tumor when he was 10 years old? Why or why not?

_____

_____

_____

5. If you were named the tallest person in the world, how would you feel? Why?

_____

_____

_____

■ Choose one statement. Then, explain why you agree or disagree.

   A. It would be fun to be the tallest person in the world.
   B. People should feel sorry for Sultan Kosen.
   C. It would be easier to be very tall than very short.

REVIEW: ENGINEERING, SCIENCE & THE BODY

■ **Use the clues to complete the crossword puzzle. Choose your answers from the word bank.**

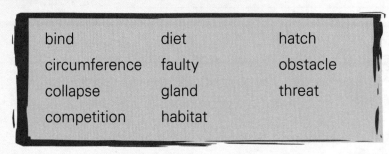

bind	diet	hatch
circumference	faulty	obstacle
collapse	gland	threat
competition	habitat	

ACROSS

6. something that blocks a path

7. what you eat

9. fasten together

10. the distance around the outside edge of a circle

11. Something that does not work correctly is _____.

DOWN

1. to cave in

2. Sultan Kosen had a tumor that pressed on his growth _____.

3. _____ occurs when many people try to win the same prize.

4. place where an animal normally lives

8. a danger or hazard

9. a small door

Name_____ Date_____

REVIEW: ENGINEERING, SCIENCE & THE BODY

■ **Circle each correct word choice.**

Some world records do not take long to set. For example, it only takes a few

seconds for Ilker Yilmaz (Turkey) to squirt milk out of his **(eye , shoe)**. Compare that to

the team in Canada that built an igloo from ice. It took them 50 hours to make the world's

(Warmest , Largest) Dome Igloo. Then, there is Xie Qiuping (China). She spent more than

35 years growing her **(garden , hair)**!

Nature deserves the credit for some world records. That is true for the record held by

Garry Turner (United Kingdom). He just happened to be born with the world's Stretchiest

(Skin , Fingers). Sultan Kosen (Turkey) is another example. A tumor caused him to grow into

the world's **(Tallest , Strongest)** Living Man. Gee Geronimo is another product of nature. This

creature naturally grew into the world's Largest **(Snail , Bird)**.

Other records are the result of human effort. Bob and Marilyn Chandler (USA) worked

hard to create the world's Largest Monster **(Ball , Truck)**. Bird lovers in the United Kingdom

worked hard to set their record. They built the world's Largest **(Birdhouse , Bird Feeder)**. Jake

Lonsway (USA) may be young, but he worked hard for his record too. He is the boy who set

the record for the world's Largest Ball of **(Plastic Wrap , String)**.

OLYMPIA THE SNOWMAN

■ Read the passage.
Tallest Snowman, February 26, 2008

If you live where it snows, you have probably built a snowman. That is a fun thing to do. The people of Bethel, Maine, know all about building snowmen. In 1999, the people in this town built the tallest snowman ever. Nine years later, they made an even bigger one. It was another Guinness World Records™ record. This new snowman was 122 feet 1 inch (37.21 m) tall!

The new snowman was called "Olympia." This was in honor of Olympia Snowe, a United States senator from Maine. So, it was not really a snowman at all. It was a snowwoman! Everyone pitched in to help build her. For example, children had the job of painting her nose orange. It took the town about a month to finish making her.

Decorating Olympia was fun too. Her eyes were made from 5-foot (1.5-m) wreaths. Her eyelashes came from 16 old skis. To make her lips, children painted five car tires bright red. Olympia had three truck tires for buttons and a 130-foot (39.6-m) scarf. People used 2,000 feet (610 m) of yellow rope for hair. Then, they put a **fleece** hat on her head. It measured 48 feet (15 m) around. When they finished, Olympia was not just a big snowwoman. She was beautiful too!

58

Name_____ Date_____

■ Answer the questions.

1. The people of Bethel, Maine, named Olympia after a
   - A. town in Greece.
   - B. U.S. senator.
   - C. hat company.

2. In this passage, the word **fleece** means _____ .
   Give an example of something you might make out of fleece.

   _____

   _____

3. Olympia was very tall. What other words would you use to describe her?

   _____

   _____

4. The author says that Olympia "was not really a snowman at all." What do you think
   this means?
   - A. The author is making a joke.
   - B. The record belongs to someone else.
   - C. The people of Bethel made a mistake.

5. Why do you think so many people helped build Olympia?

   _____

   _____

■ Choose one extension activity.

A. Make plans to build a class snowman. If you live where there is no snow, imagine
   that your class can travel to a snowy place. What materials would you use? How
   long do you think it will take to build? What different jobs will
   each member of the class have?

B. Imagine what Olympia looked like as she started to melt.
   Draw a picture to show this.

THE MANY USES OF A LEMON

■ Read the passage.

Heaviest Lemon, January 8, 2003

How big can a lemon get? Imagine a lemon the size of a large watermelon. That is how big one lemon grew. This lemon was grown in Israel. It set the Guinness World Records™ record for the Heaviest Lemon ever. It weighed 11 pounds 9.7 ounces (5.265 kg). That is heavier than most newborn babies!

Lemons grow on trees, like oranges and apples. But, people do not eat them the same way. They are too sour. Yet, lemons are used to flavor foods and make lemonade. Lemon juice is also a strong stain remover. Mixed with salt, it can clean the bottom of a cooking pot. Lemon oil can be used as a polish. It is also an **ingredient** in soaps and lotions.

Lemon juice is rich in vitamin C. Mixed with water, lemon juice may help an upset stomach. It might also help **relieve** a high fever, a sore throat, or a headache. As you can see, a lemon of any size is a very useful fruit.

DID YOU KNOW?

Although lemons have many uses, some people have a bad opinion of them. That is because of their sour taste. There is an old saying, "When life gives you lemons, make lemonade." In other words, when life gives us something bad, turn it into something good.

Name_____ Date_____

■ Answer the questions.

1. The heaviest lemon on record was the size of a large _____.

2. Lemon is used to flavor food. Name three foods that can be lemon flavored.

   _____

   _____

3. In this passage, the word **relieve** means:
   - **A.** strengthen
   - **B.** identify
   - **C.** help

4. What does **ingredient** mean? Name three ingredients in your favorite food.

   _____

   _____

5. When mixed with water, lemon juice may help an upset stomach. What do you do to help an upset stomach?

   _____

   _____

■ Choose one extension activity.

A. Make your own recipe for lemonade. How many lemons do you use? How much water? How much sugar? Share your lemonade with your family to see if they like it.

B. Create your own stain remover with lemon and water. Ask an adult if you can test it to see if it really will remove a stain. Report your findings to the class.

C. Draw a picture to illustrate the expression, "When life gives you lemons, make lemonade."

IT'S A LONG WAY DOWN

■ Read the passage.
Highest Waterfall

The Highest Waterfall in the world is Angel Falls in Venezuela, South America. It is 3,212 feet (979 m) tall, which is almost two-thirds of a mile (1 km). Angel Falls is much higher than Niagara Falls. In fact, it is about 17 times higher!

Angel Falls starts at the top of a mesa. This is a special sort of mountain named after the Spanish word for table. A mesa has a flat top. Its sides are **vertical**.

The mesa at Angel Falls is made of sandstone. It was formed billions of years ago. Its sides are slowly being washed away by rain and falling water.

Something interesting happens to the water as it tumbles down this mountain. Some of the water drops turn into mist. People can feel this mist 1 mile (1.6 km) away!

Angel Falls is named for Jimmie Angel. He was a pilot from the United States. Angel flew over the waterfall in 1933. Four years later, he flew over it again. This time he had three friends with him. Angel landed his plane on top of the mesa. His plane got stuck in the soft ground. He could not get it out. Angel and his friends had to climb down the mountain. It took them 11 days. News of their adventure soon spread. That is how the waterfall became known as Angel Falls.

Name_____ Date_____

■ Answer the questions.

1. Circle *T* for true or *F* for false.

Angel Falls is named after an American pilot.   **T**   **F**

2. On the way down the mountain, some water drops turn into
- **A.** ice.
- **B.** mist.
- **C.** steam.

3. What does **vertical** mean? Find an example of something vertical in your classroom.

_____

_____

4. Why do you think it took Angel and his friends so long to climb down the mountain?

_____

_____

5. An adjective is a word that describes something. *Sleepy* and *beautiful* are examples of adjectives. Choose three adjectives to describe Jimmie Angel. Explain why you think they fit him.

_____

_____

■ Choose one extension activity.

A. Find out more about Angel Falls and the country of Venezuela. Where in the country is this waterfall? What are the nearest cities? What rivers, mountains, or other landmarks are nearby?

B. Working in a small group, find out five facts about another famous waterfall, such as Niagara Falls or Victoria Falls. Share your facts with other groups.

WATCH IT GROW

■ Read the passage.
Fastest Growing Plant

Bamboo is the Fastest Growing Plant in the world. You can almost watch it grow! Certain species of bamboo grow up to 36 inches (91 cm) a day. That is more than 1 inch (2.5 cm) every hour! No tree grows this fast. This rapid growth makes bamboo easy to harvest in a short amount of time.

Bamboo is a member of the grass family. It grows best in **tropical** regions. Bamboo is found in Asia, North America, South America, and Africa. It is extremely useful. Some hard types of bamboo are used to make knives and arrows. Other types are tender enough to eat. Still others are so thick that they can be cut and used as water pipes. Bamboo is used to make chairs, wind chimes, fishing poles, and window shades. The list goes on and on.

Bamboo is also an excellent building material. It is really strong. It is even stronger than some kinds of steel. A bridge over a river in China is nearly the length of three football fields. The bridge does not use one nail or piece of iron. It is held up by nothing but bamboo cables. Entire homes have been built out of the stems of bamboo. Bamboo truly is an awesome blade of grass!

DID YOU KNOW?
In 1879, Thomas Edison invented the light bulb. This bulb created light by having electricity flow through a thin strip of bamboo. This light bulb is now on display at the Smithsonian Institution in Washington, D.C.

■ **Answer the questions.**

1. Bamboo is found
   A. only in Asia.
   B. in Asia, North America, South America, and Africa.
   C. on every continent.

2. According to the passage, what is something that can be made with hard bamboo?

   _____

   _____

3. What does **tropical** mean? Do you live in a tropical climate?

   _____

   _____

4. Why do you think the author believes it is important to say that the bridge in China "does not use one nail or piece of iron"?

   _____

   _____

■ **Choose one statement. Then, explain why you agree or disagree.**

A. People should be encouraged to build their homes out of bamboo.
B. Plants that grow quickly are better than plants that grow slowly.
C. More people in the United States should become bamboo farmers.

ONE AMAZING PLANT

■ Read the passage.
Largest Tomato Plant, March 27, 2007

   A scientist from Florida traveled to China. There, he found a unique tomato plant. It grew very large. The scientist took a few seeds from the plant. He brought them back to Florida. He planted them in a special greenhouse there. The tomato plants grew well in the greenhouse. One in particular grew and grew. It grew to be the world's Largest Tomato Plant. The plant covers 610.63 square feet (56.73 square m). That is about the size of a two-car garage! This tomato plant is more than just leaves and stems. It produces its own crop. This one plant **yields** about 32,000 golf-ball-sized tomatoes.

   Most people today love tomatoes. That was not always the case. For a long time, people did not dare eat them. They thought that tomatoes were **toxic**. People only grew the plants because they looked pretty in gardens. According to legend, a man named Robert Gibbon Johnson finally proved that tomatoes were safe. It is said that, in 1820, he stood on the steps of a New Jersey building. As people watched, he ate a tomato. He did not die. He did not even get sick. He showed people that tomatoes were safe. Today, people around the world know tomatoes are a safe and healthy food.

Name_____ Date_____

■ Answer the questions.

1. Circle *T* for true or *F* for false.

The Largest Tomato Plant on record is about the size
of a football field.   **T   F**

2. The seeds that grew this large plant came from the country of _____ .

3. What does **toxic** mean? Give an example of something that is toxic to humans.

_____

_____

4. In this passage, what does the word **yields** mean? What other meaning does this word have?

_____

_____

5. Many people watched Robert Gibbon Johnson eat a tomato. What expression best
explains their reaction?
   A. Seeing is believing.
   B. What goes up must come down.
   C. Saved by the bell.

6. Do you think this record-breaking tomato plant is well cared for? Explain your answer.

_____

_____

■ Choose one extension activity.

A. Find three recipes that feature tomatoes as an ingredient. Do you think you could still
make the dish if you had no tomatoes? What other ingredients, if any, could be used
in place of the tomatoes?

B. Write a short speech to convince people that tomatoes are safe to eat.

"ONE SMALL STEP FOR MAN"

■ Read the passage.
Earliest Men on the Moon, July 20, 1969

July 20, 1969, was a great day in history. On that day, Neil Armstrong (USA) became the first person to walk on the moon. Minutes later, he was followed by Edwin "Buzz" Aldrin (USA). The two men stepped out of a **lunar** landing vehicle. It was named the *Eagle*. The men were part of a United States mission. Its goal was to put a man on the moon. The mission was called *Apollo 11*.

> **DID YOU KNOW?**
> While on the moon, the two men also placed an American flag. It did not remain standing for long, however. It fell down as the *Eagle* was leaving. The blast from the rocket exhaust knocked it down.

The *Apollo 11* spacecraft had blasted off from Florida. Three men were aboard. It took them five days to reach the moon. Then, Armstrong and Aldrin left the main spacecraft. They took the *Eagle* down to the surface of the moon. Back on Earth, people watched on TV as Armstrong took his first step. He said, "That's one small step for man, one giant leap for mankind." Those are the most famous words in the history of space travel.

Armstrong and Aldrin spent 21 hours on the moon. They ran some tests. They took samples of dust and rock. Then, they went back to the *Eagle*. They returned to the main spacecraft. *Apollo 11* was a huge success for the United States space program.

■ Answer the questions.

1. Circle *T* for true or *F* for false.

   Three men from *Apollo 11* walked on the moon.   **T**   **F**

2. While on the moon, the men gathered some
   - **A.** plants.
   - **B.** water.
   - **C.** dust and rocks.

3. In Latin, the word for sun is "sol." That is why "solar" means something that relates to the sun. In Latin, the word for moon is "luna." So, what do you think **lunar** means?

   _____

   _____

4. Do you think that *Eagle* was a good name for the lunar landing vehicle? Why or why not?

   _____

   _____

5. Why do you think the author describes the day of the moon landing as "a great day in history"? Do you agree with this opinion? Why or why not?

   _____

   _____

■ Choose one statement. Then, explain why you agree or disagree.

- **A.** Exploring space is a good use of a country's money.
- **B.** Watching TV is a great way to witness important events.
- **C.** People should not take anything from the moon and bring it to Earth.

SPIDERS IN SPACE

■ Read the passage.

Earliest Spiderweb in Space, 1973

Judy Miles, a high school student, had a great idea. She wanted to see how spiders would act in space. In space, people and things float around. Could they spin webs while weightless? Miles sent her idea to NASA. NASA is the U.S. space agency. Scientists there liked her question and decided to find the answer. They blasted two spiders into **orbit** aboard a space station. These spiders became part of a mission called *Skylab 3*. Scientists named the spiders Anita and Arabella. Did they spin webs in space? Yes! This was a Guinness World Records™ achievement.

Neither spider seemed to like being weightless. After a day, Arabella did make a web. However, it was uneven and sloppy. She and Anita needed more time to get used to being in space. After a few more days, they both did better. They spun webs much the way they always did. There were some tiny differences. The webs were finer. There also were changes in thickness. Some parts of the webs were thinner than others. Still, the patterns were like those spun on Earth. Sadly, both spiders died before returning. They did not drink enough water. Their bodies dried out. Their bodies are now at a museum in Washington, D.C. These two spiders are remembered as the first eight-legged space heroes.

Name_____ Date_____

■ **Answer the questions.**

1. Circle *T* for true or *F* for false.

   Judy Miles was a space scientist who wanted
   to perform weightlessness tests on spiders.   **T**   **F**

2. In this passage, the word **orbit** means:
   - **A.** a circular path around something in space
   - **B.** the part of a spacecraft where astronauts sit
   - **C.** a short period of moving very slowly

3. How would you describe Arabella's first space web?

   _____

   _____

4. What information does the author give to suggest that neither spider liked being weightless?

   _____

   _____

5. Most spiders are not given names. Why do you think these two spiders were named?

   _____

   _____

■ **Choose one extension activity.**

   A. Judy Miles had the idea to send spiders into space. Write a paragraph
   describing an experiment that you would like scientists to conduct. What
   information might be gained by your experiment?

   B. How might it feel to be weightless? Write a poem to describe the feeling.

ALL THE LUCK IN THE WORLD

■ Read the passage.

Clover—Most Leaves, May 25, 2002

Clover is a plant with heart-shaped leaves. Almost all clover plants have three leaves. It is rare to find one with four leaves. Some people think that finding a four-leaf clover is good luck. A man from Japan actually found a clover with 18 leaves! That is a world record.

The idea that clover can bring good luck goes back hundreds of years. In 1620, Sir John Melton wrote about it. He said that anyone finding a four-leaf clover would soon "find some good thing."

Some people love clover. They mix clover plants in with the grass on their lawns. They might even **omit** the grass and cover their entire lawns with clover. Clover is easy to take care of. It has a deep green color, and it is soft to walk on. Clover is also easy to mow. Other people think of clover as a weed. These people prefer grass. They point out that clover is a delicate plant. It does not hold up well with lots of people walking on it. Also, clover attracts bees. Bees can sting people. Finally, clover will stain clothes. Whether or not you want clover on your lawn, four-leaf clovers remain a symbol of good luck. People like looking for them. It is always nice to think that some good thing may be coming your way.

DID YOU KNOW?

According to an old belief, each leaf on a clover has its own meaning. The first leaf stands for faith. The second leaf represents hope. The third leaf stands for love. The fourth leaf, of course, is for luck.

Name_____ Date_____

■ Answer the questions.

1. Some people think that a four-leaf clover is a sign of _____.

2. Name three reasons why people like to have clover on their lawns.

   _____

   _____

3. In this passage, the word **omit** means:
   - **A.** to increase
   - **B.** to leave out
   - **C.** to change

4. Sir John Melton wrote about finding "some good thing." Write about some good thing that you have found.

   _____

   _____

5. Think about the meaning people have given to each leaf of a four-leaf clover: faith, hope, love, and luck. If you found a five-leaf clover, what meaning would you give the fifth leaf? Explain your answer.

   _____

   _____

■ Choose one extension activity.

   A. See if you can find a clover growing in your area. Dry this clover by pressing it between two sheets of paper. When it dries, mount it and make a frame or border to go around it.

   B. Make a list of places in your community that you think could look nicer with clover. Explain how clover would improve the appearance of each place.

A TREE NAMED GENERAL SHERMAN

GENERAL SHERMAN

■ Read the passage.
Largest Living Tree, 2002

Redwood trees are the largest trees in the world. They are taller than the Statue of Liberty. The two kinds of redwoods are coastal redwoods and giant sequoias. Coastal redwoods are taller, but giant sequoias are larger. That is because of their **massive** volume. The largest living giant sequoia is named General Sherman. It is growing in California. It has a diameter of over 27 feet (8.2 m). That is wider than a two-lane road! Its full weight, with the roots, is about four million pounds, or almost two million kilograms! That is as much as 1,000 family cars. If you cut up General Sherman, you would get enough wood to make five billion wooden matches. That is almost one match for every person alive today!

Giant sequoias live a long time. General Sherman is about 2,100 years old. Its bark is really thick. It is 2 feet (61 cm) deep in places. Some of its branches are more than 50 feet (15.24 m) long. That is larger than many whole trees! This giant sequoia is truly one of the wonders of nature.

DID YOU KNOW?
The giant sequoia is named for a famous Native American. His name was Sequoyah. He was a member of the Cherokee nation. In 1821, he created an alphabet for his people. The alphabet helped the Cherokee people read, write, and record their history.

74

Name_____ Date_____

■ Answer the questions.

1. The largest tree in the world is the
   A. coastal redwood.
   B. giant sequoia.
   C. red oak.

2. Circle *T* for true or *F* for false.

   The giant sequoia General Sherman is found in California.   **T**   **F**

3. What does **massive** mean? What is something in your neighborhood that is massive?

   _____

   _____

4. Do you think giant sequoias would grow to be so big if they lived shorter lives? Why or why not?

   _____

   _____

5. The author calls General Sherman "one of the wonders of nature." What else would you consider to be a wonder of nature?

   _____

   _____

■ Choose one extension activity.

A. Design a birdhouse that you think would be suitable to hang on General Sherman.
B. Imagine standing at the base of General Sherman and looking up toward its uppermost branches. Write a paragraph describing how you would feel.

PRAIRIE DOG TOWN

■ Read the passage.
Largest Colony of Mammals, 1901

Prairie dogs live in large groups called towns. These towns usually have many hundreds of animals. They can cover up to 0.5 square miles (1.3 square km). Some prairie dog towns are even bigger. The largest one ever was found in 1901. It covered the ground from Texas to Mexico. About 400 million prairie dogs lived in it. That is more than all of the people in the United States. This town covered 23,705 square miles (61,400 square km). That means that it was almost the size of West Virginia!

Prairie dogs live in tunnels that go several feet under the ground. They have many rooms. There are bedrooms that are lined with dried grass. There are rooms for babies. There are even underground "toilets"! The tunnels have many entrances. Each is marked by a pile of dirt. Prairie dogs use the piles as lookouts. They watch for **predators** such as foxes and owls.

A prairie dog is about the size of a football. Prairie dogs have large eyes. They have small ears and short tails. Not everyone likes them. Many farmers do not. That is because prairie dogs eat the grass that is for cattle and horses. They also eat crops that are meant for humans. Still, most people think that prairie dogs are pretty cute.

DID YOU KNOW?
Prairie dogs are named for the sound they make. If danger is near, they give a warning bark. It sounds almost like the bark of a dog.

Name_____ Date_____

■ **Answer the questions.**

1. The biggest prairie dog town ever was almost the size of
    A. West Virginia.
    B. Mexico.
    C. Texas.

2. What kinds of rooms would you find in a prairie dog town?
    _____
    _____

3. What are **predators**? Give an example of an animal and its predator in your area.
    _____
    _____

4. Do you think that a prairie dog would prefer to live alone or with others? Explain why.
    _____
    _____

■ **Choose one statement. Then, explain why you agree or disagree.**
    A. Farmers should be more forgiving of prairie dogs.
    B. Prairie dogs should not be allowed to set up homes near farmers' crops.
    C. Prairie dogs belong in zoos.

RACING ON A RUBBER BALL

■ Read the passage.

Fastest 100 Meters on a Space Hopper—Female, September 26, 2004

Dee McDougall (United Kingdom) covered 100 meters (328 feet) in a record 39.88 seconds. You might ask, "Why is that a big deal?" After all, top runners can do it in about 11 seconds. What made McDougall's time so **noteworthy**? The answer is that she did it while sitting on a giant rubber ball! There is no record of anyone bouncing 100 meters any faster.

The ball that she used is called by many names. In the United States, it is often known as a hoppity hop. In other places, people call it a bouncer or a kangaroo ball. In the United Kingdom, people call it a space hopper. It is basically just a huge rubber ball with handles. It comes in a range of sizes. A small one might be 16 inches (41 cm) across. An adult-sized one might be 47 inches (119 cm). So, it could be the size of a small beach ball or a very large one. The first ones were either blue or red. Today, they come in all sorts of colors.

The goal is to sit on top of the ball and hop around. All you need to do is grab the handles. Then, just begin to bounce. It is possible to fall off the ball. You might skin your knee. Still, these balls are pretty safe toys. Also, they do not break easily. In fact, they are so strong that they can support 600 pounds (272 kg)! Moms, dads, and kids can go hopping through the neighborhood.

■ Answer the questions.

1. Circle *T* for true or *F* for false.

   Space hoppers are made of rubber.   **T**   **F**

2. What are two other names for space hoppers?

   _____

   _____

3. What does **noteworthy** mean? What is something noteworthy that has happened recently in your neighborhood or school?

   _____

   _____

4. Why do you think space hoppers are made in adult sizes?

   _____

   _____

5. What is another material that you think space hoppers could be made out of? Why?

   _____

   _____

■ Choose one extension activity.

A. Design an obstacle course for a space hopper. Compare your designs with those of classmates.

B. The space hopper has several names. Write your own list of names for the toy. Explain how you thought of each one.

REVIEW: EARTH EXTREMES

■ **Read each clue. Then, choose a word from the word bank to fill in the blanks. The letters in the boxes will spell what this book is about.**

fleece	noteworthy	relieve	yields
ingredient	omit	toxic	
lunar	orbit	tropical	
massive	predators	vertical	

1. something relating to the moon ___ ___ ___ ___ ☐

2. deserving attention ___ ___ ☐ ___ ___ ___ ___ ___ ___

3. a soft, warm fabric ___ ___ ___ ☐ ___ ___

4. leave out ☐ ___ ___ ___

5. hot and humid ___ ☐ ___ ___ ___ ___ ___ ___

6. creatures that prey on another creature ___ ___ ___ ☐ ___ ___ ___ ___ ___

7. large and heavy ___ ___ ☐ ___ ___ ___ ___

8. soothe or help ___ ___ ___ ___ ☐ ___ ___

9. poisonous ☐ ___ ___ ___ ___

10. a circular path around something in space ___ ___ ___ ☐ ___

11. something that is added to a mixture ___ ___ ___ ___ ___ ___ ___ ☐ ___

12. standing straight up from the ground ___ ___ ☐ ___ ___ ___ ___ ___

13. produces ___ ___ ___ ☐ ___ ___

What do the letters in the boxes spell? _____

REVIEW: EARTH EXTREMES

■ **Match the descriptions on the left with the items on the right.**

_____ 1. first man on the moon

A. Arabella

_____ 2. fastest growing plant

B. General Sherman

_____ 3. one of the first spiders in space

C. Florida

_____ 4. largest living tree

D. four-leaf clover

_____ 5. said to bring good luck

E. Olympia

_____ 6. another name for a hoppity hop

F. space hopper

_____ 7. largest snowman

G. prairie dogs

_____ 8. highest waterfall

H. Neil Armstrong

_____ 9. rich in vitamin C

I. lemon

_____ 10. formed the largest colony of mammals

J. Angel Falls

_____ 11. home of the world's largest tomato plant

K. bamboo

FANTASY SKATEBOARD

■ Read the passage.
Largest Skateboard, February 25, 2009

Most skateboards are not much longer than your arm. They are just big enough for one person. But, not this skateboard! In 2009, Rob Dyrdek (USA) built a skateboard that is 36 feet 7 inches (11.14 m) long. That is about as long as three cars! The board is 8 feet 8 inches (2.63 m) wide and more than 3 feet 7.5 inches (1.1 m) high.

Dyrdek built the board on his reality TV show. The show is called *Rob Dyrdek's* **Fantasy Factory**. Dyrdek's giant skateboard looks just like a regular skateboard. The difference is its size. It is big enough for many people to ride at once. It has even been ridden during parades.

Dyrdek has loved skateboards since he was a boy. He started riding when he was 12. A few years later, he turned pro. Today, Dyrdek enjoys his TV show. Beyond that, he tries to help the sport that he loves. He wants to encourage young riders. That is why he has helped build skateboard parks across the country. Dyrdek makes sure that the parks are safe and legal. And, of course, he makes them fun.

Name_____ Date_____

■ Answer the questions.

1. Circle *T* for true or *F* for false.

   Dyrdek did not begin riding a skateboard until he
   was an adult.   **T**   **F**

2. Dyrdek built the world's largest skateboard
   - **A.** in his garage.
   - **B.** in a playground.
   - **C.** on his TV show.

3. In this passage, **fantasy** means *a product of the imagination*. What
   would be an antonym (the opposite) of fantasy?

   _____

   _____

4. Skateboarding is a sport that requires riding on something. Name
   three other sports that require riding and tell what is being ridden.

   _____

   _____

5. Do you think that skateboarders should be allowed to ride on streets and sidewalks or only in
   skateboard parks? Why?

   _____

   _____

■ Choose one extension activity.

- **A.** Draw a design for a new skateboard park in your community. Be sure to include the
  measurements of the park and its features.
- **B.** Design your own TV show. Tell what the show would be about and who would star on it.

NOSE SPINNING TRICK

■ **Read the passage.**
Longest Duration Spinning a Basketball on the Nose, February 13, 2010

Spinning a basketball on the tip of your finger is hard to do. Still, many people do learn to do it. It just takes practice. Spinning the ball on your head is much more challenging. Only a few people can do that. Spinning the ball on your nose is even harder. Keep that in mind as you read about Scooter Christensen (USA). He is a professional basketball player. He plays for the Harlem Globetrotters. Christensen holds two spinning records. He once spun a ball on his head for 6 seconds. He also holds the record for spinning a ball on his nose. He did that for 5.1 seconds. That is a full second more than the old record.

As a boy, Christensen loved soccer. When he grew taller than most boys, he turned to basketball. He was a basketball star in high school. He was also a sports star in college. He tried out for the Phoenix Suns, but he did not make the team. Then, one day, he was playing a pickup game. A **scout** for the Harlem Globetrotters spotted him. The scout liked what he saw. He invited Christensen to try out for the Globetrotters.

Christensen made the team. Since then, he has traveled with the Globetrotters all over the world. The team calls itself the "Magicians of Basketball." They do all kinds of funny tricks and fancy plays. People love to watch them. Scooter Christensen is now one of the team's stars.

Name_____ Date_____

■ **Answer the questions.**

1. Circle *T* for true or *F* for false.

   Christensen played basketball in high school and college.   **T**   **F**

2. In this passage, the word **scout** means:
   A. a spy
   B. the member of a service organization
   C. someone searching for talent

3. Why do you think it is so hard to spin a basketball on your nose?

   _____

   _____

4. Do you think the Harlem Globetrotters are real magicians? Why do the Globetrotters call themselves the "Magicians of Basketball?"

   _____

   _____

5. Based on this passage, would you like to be a Harlem Globetrotter? Why or why not?

   _____

   _____

■ **Choose one statement. Then, explain why you agree or disagree.**
   A. Basketball is a better game than soccer.
   B. It is important for kids to play sports.
   C. Basketball is a fun sport to watch.

A HOUSE WITH MANY KINGS AND QUEENS

■ Read the passage.
**Tallest House of Cards,
October 16, 2007**

Imagine trying to build a house out of playing cards. It isn't easy. Many people try it once or twice. Then, they give up. It is not easy to build more than two or three levels. Then, the house usually collapses. Bryan Berg (USA) knows this. But, Berg does not give up. As a result, he has become a master card builder. In 2007, he **constructed** a huge house of cards. It was 25 feet 9.4 inches (7.86 m) high. That is taller than a two-story building! This new world record house took him five weeks and 1,800 decks of cards to finish.

Berg built his first house of cards when he was eight years old. He liked the challenge. He tried different designs to build his card houses higher and higher. Berg says he felt a "magical feeling" whenever his houses got close to the ceiling. In 1992, at age 17, Berg broke the world record. His tower of cards reached 14 feet 6 inches (4.42 m).

Bryan Berg has been going higher and higher ever since. He builds all his houses without glue or tape. At any time, a gust of wind could blow the cards down. That is why he builds his houses in a space with no windows. Could he someday build a house of cards 100 feet (30 m) high? "Sure," he says, "but it's going to take a while."

DID YOU KNOW?

Playing cards have been around for many hundreds of years. No one knows for sure where or when they were invented. It is likely that they come from China. Today, people around the world use English playing cards. These have 52 cards and two jokers. Still, other types of decks remain. In Italy, they use a pack with just 40 cards. In Russia, they use 36 cards. In India, cards are round instead of rectangular.

Name_____ Date_____

■ Answer the questions.

1. Circle *T* for true or *F* for false.

Bryan Berg holds his card houses together using only glue and tape.   **T   F**

2. Why does Berg build his card houses in a room with no windows?

_____

_____

3. In this passage, the word **constructed** means:
   A. built
   B. designed
   C. purchased

4. Has any achievement ever given you a "magical feeling?" If so, what?

_____

_____

5. Name three things that could cause a house of cards to fall down.

_____

_____

6. Bryan Berg is great at building card houses. Do you think this means that he would be great at building real houses? Why or why not?

_____

_____

■ Choose one extension activity.

A. Working in small groups, try to build a tall tower out of blocks. See how high you can go before it tips over. Compare your record to that of other groups.

B. Write a poem describing the "magical feeling" of building a very tall house of cards.

AN UNDERWATER BIKE RIDE

■ Read the passage.
Deepest Cycling Underwater, July 21, 2008

Most people who break sports records are young. Vittorio Innocente (Italy) was different. He was 62 years old when he broke the world record for the deepest cycling underwater. Whose record did he break? He smashed his own record set three years earlier. This second time he went down 214 feet 10 inches (66.5 m). That is like going down 20 sets of stairs!

How did he do it? First, he put on scuba diving gear to help him breathe underwater. With help from other scuba divers, he was able to **descend** to the ocean floor. At 92 feet (28 m), the ocean floor sloped away and went even deeper. Innocente got on his mountain bike and began pedaling. He had to be careful of mud pools and large rocks in his path. It took nine minutes to reach the record depth.

Innocente made his wild ride for two reasons. He wanted to raise money for charity. Also, he wanted to prove that mountain bikes can go anywhere, maybe even the surface of the moon!

DID YOU KNOW?
How did Innocente get the idea to become an underwater cyclist? It came to him when he was a young man. He was scuba diving with a group of people. One of them saw an old bicycle lying on the ocean floor. The diver picked it up and began to ride it. That was when Innocente decided to combine his love of diving with his love of cycling.

88

Name_____ Date_____

■ Answer the questions.

1. Innocente made his ride partly to raise money for _____ .

2. Why did Innocente need scuba diving gear?

   _____

   _____

3. An antonym is the opposite of a word. Which is an antonym of **descend**?
   - **A.** shout
   - **B.** start
   - **C.** go up

4. Describe the challenges that Innocente faced as he rode down the underwater slope.

   _____

   _____

5. Why do you think the author calls it a "wild ride"?

   _____

   _____

■ Choose one statement. Then, explain why you agree or disagree.
- **A.** Biking deep underwater is a dangerous thing to do.
- **B.** People should not go in the ocean and disturb the creatures there just to set this kind of record.
- **C.** More older people should do what Vittorio Innocente has done.

RUNNING ON STILTS

■ **Read the passage.**
Fastest Marathon on Stilts, April 13, 2008

Michelle Frost (United Kingdom) was the tallest runner in the marathon. No other runner was close. She was taller than the tallest man. She did have a little boost, however. Frost ran on 4-foot (1.2-m) stilts! She ran the 26 mile 385 yard (42.2 km) race in 8 hours, 25 minutes. That was a new Guinness World Records™ record. This marathon was held in London, England. Over 35,000 runners **participated** in the race. Frost finished more than six hours behind the winner. But, she had the best view of the race!

Frost had learned to walk on stilts eight years earlier. Still, running on stilts was a new challenge. She wanted to raise money for charity. She thought that running a marathon on stilts might help. To prepare for the race, she trained hard. She fell several times. Fortunately, she trained on grass. In the marathon, she ran on paved streets. Any fall during the race would have really hurt. Somehow, she made it without falling.

Frost was sore at the finish. She had several bruises and blisters. "They soon heal," she said after the race. Frost did more than set a new world record. As she hoped, her race drew lots of attention. She raised over $10,000 for charity. It was a great effort all around.

DID YOU KNOW?

The marathon used to be exactly 26 miles (24 km). But, that changed in 1908. In that year, the Olympic Games were held in London. The Royal Family wanted a better view of the finish, so race officials added 385 yards (352 m). That put the finish line right in front of the Royal box seats. The extra distance became a permanent addition.

Name_____ Date_____

■ Answer the questions.

1. Circle *T* for true or *F* for false.

   Michelle Frost took several bad falls during the marathon.   **T**   **F**

2. **Participated** means _____.

3. Why do you think Michelle Frost trained on grass instead of pavement?

   _____

   _____

4. What information in this passage suggests that running on stilts is not quite the same as walking on stilts?

   _____

   _____

5. Do you think Frost was disappointed to finish more than six hours behind the winner? Why or why not?

   _____

   _____

■ Choose one extension activity.

A. Imagine that you want to raise money for your favorite charity. You might not be able to run a marathon on stilts, but think of some activity you could do. Then, design a flyer asking people to support you by donating money.

B. Imagine that you are a runner who won a marathon race. Write what a sports reporter might say about you and your victory.

DOG RACING ON A BEACH

■ Read the passage.

Fastest 100 Meters Bike Sled Dog Racing on Sand with Eight Dogs, November 6, 2007

Suzannah Sorrell (United Kingdom) loves a challenge. In 2007, some people offered her thousands of dollars. The money would go to dog charities. All she had to do was break a world record with her huskies.

Huskies are a breed of dog that loves snow. But, to break the record, Sorrell used sand instead of snow. She attached her dogs to a special dog sled. Instead of having **runners**, it had wheels. Riding this "bike sled," she drove her eight dogs across a sandy beach. They went 100 meters (328 feet) in 10.65 seconds. It was a new world record. Sorrell earned the money.

As a child, Sorrell had seen a TV show about people breaking records. Now, she has an interest in it. She wants to break some records on snow in the Arctic. After all, her huskies are not sand dogs. They are snow dogs. They enjoy temperatures that drop below zero. They always stay warm because they have two coats of fur. One is a coarse outercoat. The second is a woolly undercoat. Huskies also have lots of energy. And, pulling sleds across snow or sand is a great way to release it!

DID YOU KNOW?
Have you heard the phrase "three dog night?" It was started by people who live in Arctic regions. It means a very cold night. It is so cold that you need to sleep with three dogs to keep warm.

■ Answer the questions.

1. Circle *T* for true or *F* for false.

    By setting the world record, Sorrell earned money for dog charities.   **T**   **F**

2. In what ways are huskies well-suited to cold weather?

    _____

    _____

3. In this passage, the word **runners** means:
    A. messengers
    B. blades
    C. narrow carpets

4. Based on the passage, do you think huskies would enjoy spending their days living in a city apartment? Why or why not?

    _____

    _____

5. As a child, Suzannah Sorrell watched a show on record-breakers. Have you seen someone do something on TV that you would like to do? Explain your answer.

    _____

    _____

■ Choose one statement. Then, explain why you agree or disagree.

A. It is cruel to have dogs pull a sled.
B. TV shows should not feature world record-breakers.
C. Human charities are more important than animal charities.

A HUMAN SPINNING TOP

■ Read the passage.
Most Head Spins in One Minute, December 30, 2007

In 2007, 18-year-old Aichi Ono from Japan held the record for spinning on his head. He spun around 101 times in one minute. On December 30 of that year, he broke his own world record. He spun on his head an incredible 109 times in one minute. That is almost two spins a second!

Spinning on your head is a challenging dance move. You must use your head to stand on while spinning your body around on the dance floor. It requires great strength and balance. Experts recommend that you wear a helmet or knit cap on your head when you head spin. Music would also help. A nice slick floor surface helps too. Getting those things is the easy part.

Now comes the hard part. First, you have to learn how to balance yourself on your head. This is called a headstand. Next, you must begin to spin yourself around. You do this by pushing the floor with your hands. Once you gain enough **momentum**, you stop pushing the floor and keep your hands in the air. Then, you just spin like crazy!

DID YOU KNOW?
There are two reasons that a person should wear a helmet or knit cap when head spinning. First, it will reduce friction. That means that you will spin more easily. Second, it will save your hair. If you spin a lot without some sort of head covering, it might damage your hair.

Name_____ Date_____

■ Answer the questions.

1. Circle *T* for true or *F* for false.

   Head spinning is considered a dance move.   **T**   **F**

2. If something is gaining **momentum**, it is gaining
   - **A.** wealth.
   - **B.** weight.
   - **C.** speed.

3. What action or movement can you think of that you could do 109 times in one minute?

   _____

   _____

4. Do you think that head spinning would be more popular with younger people or with older people? Why?

   _____

   _____

■ Choose one extension activity.

A. Head spinning is a form of dancing. Choose another form of dancing and research its history.

B. Aichi Ono is from Japan. What forms of dancing were done in Japan a long time ago? What forms of dancing are popular there today?

A GIANT PICKUP GAME

■ Read the passage.
Largest Game of Pick Up Sticks, July 21, 2007

Do you know where Zimbabwe is? It is a country in Africa. If you had been in Zimbabwe on July 21, 2007, you might have seen an amazing sight. On that day, a group of high school students set a new Guinness World Records™ record. They played the world's Largest Game of Pick Up Sticks ever. The sticks were a world-record size. They were 29 feet 10.3 inches (9.10 m) long. That is about as long as a telephone pole. Each one had a diameter of 5.7 inches (14.5 cm). That means that each stick was almost as big around as a gallon of paint.

Pick up sticks is an old game. People around the world have played it for hundreds of years. The rules and scoring vary from place to place. But, the idea is the same. The game is played with long sticks. The sticks are painted different colors. Each color has a certain point value. Some are worth more than others. For example, a red stick may be worth ten points. A blue stick may be worth only five points. In the United States, the game usually has 25 to 30 sticks with four or five different colors. To start the game, you hold the sticks upright. Then, you let them drop. The sticks fall at **random**. Each player then takes a turn. The goal is to pick up, or remove, a stick from the pile without moving any of the other sticks. The first player to reach a certain number of points wins.

■ Answer the questions.

1. Circle *T* for true or *F* for false.

The record for Largest Game of Pick Up Sticks was set by
elementary students.   **T   F**

2. The sticks in the world's Largest Game of Pick Up Sticks were about as long as

_____ .

3. What does **random** mean? Could pick up sticks be played if the sticks were not
dropped randomly?

_____

_____

4. In what ways do you think it would be challenging to play pick up sticks with sticks
this large?

_____

_____

5. What is your favorite game to play? What is it about this game that you like?

_____

_____

6. Is pick up sticks a game you have ever played? Does it sound like a fun game to
play? Why or why not?

_____

_____

■ Choose one extension activity.

A. Create your own set of pick up sticks. Choose something creative
to use for the sticks, such as toothpicks, twigs, pencils, etc. Give
point values to different colored sticks. Use your set to play a game
of pick up sticks with a friend.

B. Zimbabwe is where this record was set. Find Zimbabwe on
a map. Now, draw an outline of Africa and place Zimbabwe
on it. Also, label the countries that touch Zimbabwe.

ZIPPING DOWNHILL

■ Read the passage.
Fastest Speed Riding a Minibob/Zipflbob, April 11, 2009

It is called a minibob in the United States. In Europe, they call it a zipflbob. Either way, it is a fun sled. It is usually used on snow. It can also skim across grass, sand, or water. Anyone can ride one. As one group says, this sled is for "girls and boys ages five to 100." Don't let its small size fool you. These sleds can go fast! Just ask Frederick Eiter (Austria) who broke the world speed record at 97.77 miles (157.34 km) per hour!

The minibob looks like the seat of a chair. A big stick handle coming from the seat is used for steering and braking. To turn the sled, the driver holds the handle and leans one way or the other. The sled is made from plastic. It weighs just 4.5 pounds (2 kg). This makes it easy to carry up a hill.

Because these sleds are so fast, you need to control your speed. You can slow down or brake by pulling the handle back and digging your heels in the snow. Always remember this sledding **slogan**, "Ride hard, but safe!"

DID YOU KNOW?
One day you may see minibobs in the winter Olympic Games. Official minibob racing began in 1999. Four years later, the first Zipflbob World Series was held. Minibob racing has spread to five different countries, including the United States. Sometimes, riders race against the clock to see who is fastest. Other times, they race against each other in a pack.

Name_____ Date_____

■ Answer the questions.

1. The handle on a minibob is used for _____ .

2. What is a **slogan**? How is the slogan mentioned in the passage useful to people?

_____

_____

3. What is one advantage to having a sled that is light in weight?

_____

_____

4. A minibob is one way to get down a snowy slope. What other equipment could you use to get down a snowy slope?

_____

_____

5. Do you really think that 100-year-olds would use a minibob? If not, why would this sled be called a product for "girls and boys ages five to 100"?

_____

_____

_____

■ Choose one extension activity.

A. The minibob is not yet part of the Olympics, but many other winter sports are. Choose an Olympic winter sport and learn about its history.

B. Look around your community for other slogans on signs or bulletin boards. How many can you find that focus on safety? What do these slogans say?

REVIEW: GAME TIME!

■ **Find the words hidden in the puzzle. The words may be found across or down.**

constructed	momentum	runners
descend	participate	scout
fantasy	random	slogan

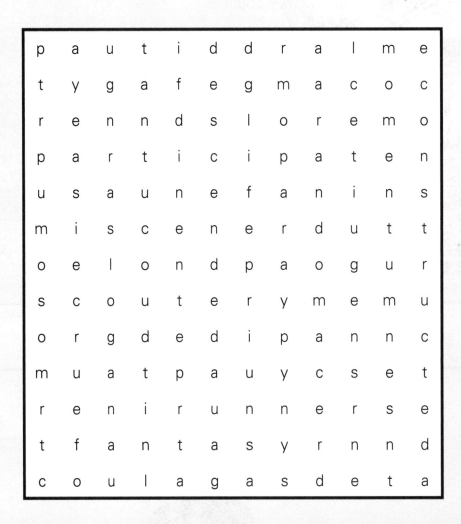

p	a	u	t	i	d	d	r	a	l	m	e
t	y	g	a	f	e	g	m	a	c	o	c
r	e	n	n	d	s	l	o	r	e	m	o
p	a	r	t	i	c	i	p	a	t	e	n
u	s	a	u	n	e	f	a	n	i	n	s
m	i	s	c	e	n	e	r	d	u	t	t
o	e	l	o	n	d	p	a	o	g	u	r
s	c	o	u	t	e	r	y	m	e	m	u
o	r	g	d	e	d	i	p	a	n	n	c
m	u	a	t	p	a	u	y	c	s	e	t
r	e	n	i	r	u	n	n	e	r	s	e
t	f	a	n	t	a	s	y	r	n	n	d
c	o	u	l	a	g	a	s	d	e	t	a

REVIEW: GAME TIME!

■ **Circle each correct word choice.**

Many unusual Guinness World Records™ records have been set in the category of

Game Time! Some people start with an ordinary sport and do something unique with it. That is

what Vittorio Innocente (Italy) did. He took a regular **(snowboard , bike)** and rode it underwater.

Michelle Frost (United Kingdom) entered a regular **(marathon , ski race)** but completed it on

stilts. Scooter Christensen (USA) started with a regular basketball. He set a record by spinning

it on his **(finger , nose)**.

Other people make changes to their equipment to set records. That is what Rob

Dyrdek (USA) did. He made the world's **(Lightest , Largest)** skateboard. High school students

in Zimbabwe made **(giant , electric)** pick up sticks. Suzannah Sorrell (United Kingdom) set a

record with her dogsled team tied to a **(boat , bike)** sled.

Finally, some people take regular sports and games and carry them to the extreme.

Aichi Ono (Japan) is an example of this. He started with a regular **(karate , dance)** move that

involved spinning on his head. He turned that into a record for the Most Head Spins in

One Minute. Frederick Eiter (Austria) went **(farther , faster)** on his minibob than anyone else

had ever gone. And, Bryan Berg (USA) built the Tallest House of **(Cards , Cups)** ever.

GOLDEN SNEAKERS

■ Read the passage.
Most Expensive Pair of Sneakers, 2007

Ken Courtney (USA) designs expensive things. In fact, he designs *very* expensive things. In 2007, he designed the world's Most Expensive Pair of Sneakers. They cost $4,053! First, he took ordinary high-top sneakers. Then, he dipped them in gold. He made five pairs. Each pair had the same **astronomical** price tag.

Courtney's sneakers are not meant for playing basketball. They are meant to be put on display. In other words, they are meant to show off. After all, only four other people in the world have sneakers like these.

Ken Courtney has made a whole collection of such items. He has dipped the cap of a ballpoint pen in gold. He has also made a gold coffee stirrer. He did this by putting gold on a cheap plastic stirrer from a fast-food restaurant. In the fashion world, Courtney is known as "Ju$t Another Rich Kid." The $ sign instead of the letter *S* is not a mistake. That is Courtney's designer name. Courtney says that his works of art are sold to people who "have everything." There may not be many folks in this category. Still, there are enough. Ken Courtney is highly successful. People from around the world buy his products.

102

Name_____ Date_____

■ Answer the questions.

1. Why are the sneakers made by Ken Courtney so expensive?

_____

_____

2. What would a person probably do with a pair of Ken Courtney's sneakers?
   A. play basketball
   B. walk around the block
   C. put them on display

3. What is the best meaning for the word **astronomical**? Write a new sentence using the word correctly.

_____

_____

4. The author of this passage says that Courtney's sneakers are meant to "show off." What can you conclude from this?
   A. The author thinks that the sneakers are purchased to impress people.
   B. The author loves the sneakers.
   C. The author wishes that the sneakers cost even more money.

5. Ken Courtney's designer name is "Ju$t Another Rich Kid." If he wanted a different name, what would you suggest?

_____

_____

6. Would you like to own something from Ken Courtney's collection? Why or why not?

_____

_____

■ Choose one extension activity.

A. Create an advertisement for a pair of Ken Courtney's sneakers. Your advertisement can be a radio ad, a newspaper ad, or a poster.

B. Think of something you own that you would like to have dipped in gold. Write a letter to Ken Courtney explaining to him why you would like this particular item coated with gold.

THAT HAS TO HURT!

■ Read the passage.

Heaviest Car Balanced on the Head, May 24, 1999

John Evans (United Kingdom) likes to puts things on his head. He has a great talent for balancing things there. He has balanced bricks on his head. He has balanced books and barrels. In 1999, he set a new world record by balancing the shell of a small Mini car on his head. The car weighed 352 pounds (159.66 kg). Evans held it up for 33 seconds.

Evans is a big man. He is 6 feet 1 inch (1.9 m) tall. He weighs 343 pounds (155.7 kg). The key to his power, however, is his neck. It is huge. It is 24 inches (60.9 cm) around. That is almost as big around as a volleyball. It is a good thing that Evans's neck is so strong. Balancing a car on your head is risky. One slip and the car would drop. Evans would have no way to protect himself.

But, Evans has not been injured practicing his hobby. He keeps on working as a "head balancer." His strong neck is ready for almost anything. He has broken 25 head-balancing records so far. He is ready for more.

DID YOU KNOW?

In 1977, the owners of Mini cars were offered a deal. A blue jeans company wanted to use Minis to advertise their jeans. The company offered to pay Mini car owners every month. All the owners had to do was let the company paint a design on their cars. The design was the company **logo** and a huge zipper. The cars then became moving advertisements.

Name_____ Date_____

■ Answer the questions.

1. John Evans is a _____ man.
   - **A.** big
   - **B.** loud
   - **C.** sneaky

2. Circle *T* for true or *F* for false.

   A **logo** is a symbol that identifies a company or product.   **T**   **F**

3. John Evans's interest in head balancing could best be described as
   - **A.** unusual.
   - **B.** mean.
   - **C.** weak.

4. Do you think that the owners of the Mini car company are happy about what John Evans does? Why or why not?

   _____

   _____

5. What item would you like to see John Evans balance on his head? Explain your answer.

   _____

   _____

■ Choose one extension activity.

- **A.** Find out more about the human neck. How many muscles are in your neck? What are their names?
- **B.** In some parts of the world, people often carry things on their heads. Find three countries where this is common. What things do people carry in these countries? How heavy might these things be?
- **C.** How much does an average car weigh? What about a truck? A motorcycle? Research to find out.

TIME FOR DESSERT

■ Read the passage.
Largest Ice Cream Cup, September 13, 2005

Anniversaries are special days. Sometimes, people celebrate in unusual ways. In 2005, an ice cream company had its 60th anniversary. To celebrate, the company tried to break a record. It wanted to make the world's Largest Ice Cream Cup. The company did it! Its "cup" took 1,289 gallons (4,879 L) of vanilla ice cream. It weighed 8,865 pounds (4,021 kg). That is about the weight of three cars.

Breaking the record was not easy. First, people had to make a giant cup and scoop ice cream into it. Six people scooped for 15 hours. As the last step, the whole thing had to be weighed. People had to do this quickly. The ice cream was starting to melt!

Two people measured the mound of ice cream. It took 20 minutes to get all of the measurements. At last, the numbers were put into a computer. It **confirmed** the new record. By then, the ice cream was melting even more. There was just one thing to do. Everyone grabbed a spoon. They began to eat.

> **DID YOU KNOW?**
> Ice cream has been around for over 2,000 years. People in ancient China ate it. So did the ancient Romans. But, Americans gave it its name. More than 200 years ago, they labeled it "iced cream." In time, the name was shortened to ice cream.

Name_____ Date_____

■ **Answer the questions.**

1. Why did the company want to set a world record?

_____

_____

2. What flavor of ice cream did the company use to set the world record?

_____

3. What does **confirmed** mean? Why is it important that a world record is confirmed?

_____

_____

4. In what way was teamwork important in breaking this record?

_____

_____

5. Do you think that this record-setting cup of ice cream can still be seen today? Why or why not?

_____

_____

■ **Choose one statement. Then, explain why you agree or disagree.**

A. You should always do something special on an anniversary.

B. It was a bad idea to waste hundreds of gallons of ice cream just to set a Guinness World Record.

C. An answer given by a computer can always be trusted.

LETTING THEM GROW

■ Read the passage.

Longest Fingernails (Female)—Ever, February 23, 2008

In 1979, Lee Redmond (USA) had a crazy idea. She decided to stop cutting her fingernails. For 30 years, she let them grow and grow. By 2008, her nails had grown to a record length. Counting all fingers, they measured 28 feet 4.5 inches (8.65 m). Her right thumb had the longest nail. It was 2 feet 11 inches (89 cm).

It must have been hard to have such long nails. Redmond, however, did not mind. How did she do everyday things? "Very carefully," she always said. Somehow, Redmond went 30 years without breaking a single nail. She took good care of them. Every day she soaked them in olive oil. She cleaned them with a toothbrush. Redmond was proud of her nails. They made her famous. Once, a TV show offered her $100,000. All she had to do was cut her nails on live TV. She said no.

Then, on February 11, 2009, Lee Redmond was **injured** in a car accident. All of her nails broke off in the accident. Her nails had been her joy. Still, she knew that she was lucky to be alive. In time, her body healed. She was still sad about her nails. But, she said, "There really is more to me than my fingernails."

DID YOU KNOW?

Fingernails grow faster in warm weather than in the cold. They also grow faster in the daytime than at night. Not all of your fingernails grow at the same rate. If you are right-handed, the fingernails on your right hand will grow faster than the fingernails on your left hand. For left-handed people, it is just the reverse.

Name_____ Date_____

■ Answer the questions.

1. Lee Redmond was offered $100,000 to _____.

2. What does the word **injured** mean? What caused Redmond to be injured?

_____

_____

3. Describe how Lee Redmond took care of her nails.

_____

_____

4. Name two things that would be hard to do with very long fingernails.

_____

_____

5. Lee Redmond said, "There really is more to me than my fingernails." In your own words, explain what you think she meant.

_____

_____

■ Choose one extension activity.

A. What are some things that fingernails can help you do? Write a poem about the uses of fingernails.

B. Write a journal entry for one day of living with nails as long as Redmond's. How would you complete everyday activities?

BIG BOLD BUNNY

■ Read the passage.
Largest Rabbit Made of Chocolate, March 30, 2009

Most people like bunnies. Most people also like chocolate. So, it makes sense to put the two together. In fact, each year about 90 million chocolate bunnies are made. In 2009, a company in Brazil made a huge chocolate rabbit. It weighed 6,172 pounds 15 ounces (2,800 kg). That set a Guinness World Records™ record. The bunny weighed one and a half times as much as a car!

The first chocolate bunny was made in Germany. That was 200 years ago. The bunny was made to celebrate spring. It was considered a sign of new life. Later, some people from Germany moved to the United States. They brought their love of chocolate bunnies with them. Soon, people in the United States were eating chocolate bunnies. Some of these bunnies were milk chocolate. Some were dark chocolate. Some were even white chocolate. People loved them all. That is why so many are sold each year.

How should you eat a chocolate rabbit? People have different thoughts on this. One study found that most people in the United States think that you should eat the ears first. Five **percent** said the feet should go first. Another four percent picked the tail. Which do you eat first? Now, think of eating the one made in Brazil. Where would you even start?

Name_____ Date_____

■ Answer the questions.

1. The first chocolate bunny was made in _____ .

2. Circle *T* for true or *F* for false.

Chocolate rabbits have been around for 400 years.   **T**   **F**

3. In this passage, the word **percent** means:
   A. a part out of one hundred
   B. an amount broken down into dollars and cents
   C. the average of all numbers in a set

4. Chocolate rabbits were originally made to celebrate spring. What other ways do people celebrate spring?

_____

_____

5. What other items made of chocolate have you seen? How do they compare to the record-setting chocolate rabbit?

_____

_____

■ Choose one extension activity.

A. Conduct a survey of your classmates to find out their favorite kinds of chocolate. How many like dark chocolate best, how many like milk chocolate best, and how many like white chocolate best? How many do not like chocolate at all? Make a chart to display your results.

B. Write a set of directions for eating a chocolate bunny. Begin with your own favorite starting point— ears, tail, or feet. Tell why it is the best place to start.

TRY WRITING WITH THIS!

■ Read the passage.
Longest Pencil, August 27, 2007

Don't worry. You will not have to take a test with this pencil. That is a good thing because you could never lift it. No one could. This pencil is the world's Longest Pencil. It is 76 feet 2.75 inches (23.23 m) long. That is about as long as a tennis court.

The idea for the pencil came from Ashrita Furman (USA). He runs a health food store in New York City, New York. He is also the world's greatest Guinness World Records™ record-breaker. Furman holds about 100 Guinness World Records.

Furman needed help to make his pencil. He gathered a team of 40 volunteers. They came from 20 countries. The team worked over 12 hours a day for two weeks. Furman did not want something that just looked like a pencil. He wanted a real pencil. He made sure the "lead" in the center was real **graphite**. This lead was 10 inches (25.4 cm) thick. It weighed 4,500 pounds (2,041 kg). That is as much as a great white shark! How could such a big pencil ever be sharpened? It was sharpened with an electric saw!

DID YOU KNOW?
Ashrita Furman has set some crazy records. He bounced underwater on a pogo stick farther than anyone. He made the world's biggest lollipop. He even set a record for Hula-hoop® racing while balancing a milk bottle on his head.

Name_____ Date_____

■ Answer the questions.

1. Circle *T* for true or *F* for false.

The world's Longest Pencil is too heavy for any person to lift.   **T   F**

2. What are two of the records Ashrita Furman has set?

_____

_____

3. What part of a pencil is made from **graphite**?

_____

4. If you were going to build something to set a world record, what would you build and why?

_____

_____

5. Do you enjoy being part of a team? Why or why not?

_____

_____

■ Choose one extension activity.

A. Write a speech that will inspire people to break world records.

B. List three questions you would like to ask
Ashrita Furman. Write the responses that
you think Furman might give.

LOOK MOM: NO HANDS!

■ Read the passage.
Largest Bubblegum Bubble Blown, April 24, 2004

It began as a hobby. In high school, Chad Fell (USA) just had a **knack** for blowing bigger bubblegum bubbles than anyone else. Later, he worked as a reporter. He wrote about local sports. He blew big bubbles at sporting events. Fans and even players cheered him on. They called him "Bubble Man." In 2004, he set a Guinness World Records™ record for blowing the Largest Bubblegum Bubble. Fell did it without using his hands in any way. His bubble was 20 inches (50.8 cm) across. That is more than twice as big as a basketball!

The rules that Guinness World Records sets are strict. To make his bubble official, Fell had to have someone make a film showing him blowing the bubble. He needed **witnesses**. He had the mayor and several other people watch him. Fell could not use more than three pieces of gum. He had to hold the bubble for five seconds. Also, he could not touch the bubble with his hands.

What is his secret? Fell says it is best to blow bubbles at room temperature. Warm air helps make bigger bubbles. In addition, he uses gum with sugar in it. He chews the gum for 15 minutes to dissolve most of the sugar. Then, he is ready. There is just one more thing. If you try to blow bubbles using Fell's secrets, make your parents and dentist happy. Brush your teeth afterwards.

DID YOU KNOW?
People have been chewing some form of gum for thousands of years. Frank Fleer invented the first bubble gum in 1906. The first baseball cards were added to gum packages in the 1930s. During World War II, American soldiers gave chewing gum as gifts to people in Europe and Asia.

■ Answer the questions.

1. Chad Fell's nickname was _____ .

2. What does the word **witnesses** mean? Name an event where you have been a witness.

_____

_____

3. If you have a **knack** for something, it means:
   A. you have a talent for it
   B. you treat it roughly
   C. you keep it in a special carrying bag

4. What rules did Fell have to follow to be named a Guinness World Record holder?

_____

_____

5. Why do you think that Guinness World Records sets such strict rules?

_____

_____

6. Why do you think the author tells you to brush your teeth after blowing bubbles like Fell?

_____

_____

■ Choose one extension activity.

A. Using gum, see how big a bubble you can blow. Have friends act as witnesses to help confirm how big your biggest bubble gets.

B. Choose a song you like and change the words so that the song is about bubblegum. Compare your "new" song to those of your classmates.

HANGING ON

■ Read the passage.
Longest Monkey Bars, May 1995

Have you ever climbed a set of monkey bars? Monkey bars are like a **horizontal** ladder. The ladder is up high, so your feet cannot touch the ground. You climb up and grab onto the first bar. Then, while hanging in the air, you grab the next bar. You swing from one bar to the next, just like a monkey. The goal is to see if you can swing all the way to the end of the bars. Most playground monkey bars have 6 to 8 bars. A big set might have 12 or 15. You must have strong arms and shoulders to make it across. Now imagine making it across the Longest Monkey Bars in the world. On this set, there are 400 bars!

These monkey bars were built in Japan in 1995. They are made of stainless steel. The bars are 39.4 inches (1 m) wide. Each bar is 20 inches (50 cm) away from the next one. At the highest point, the bars are 6 feet 8 inches (2 m) off the ground. A normal-sized adult could reach up and touch them. But, these bars are not meant for adults. They are used by school children. The bars cover a distance of 334.65 feet (102 m). That is longer than a football field. You would need super-strong arms and shoulders to make it across all 400 bars.

With most monkey bars, you might be good enough to reach the end. Then, you would wonder if you could have gone longer. With 400 bars to swing across, that would never be a problem.

Name_____ Date_____

■ Answer the questions.

1. Circle *T* for true or *F* for false.

The Longest Monkey Bars in the world have 394 bars.　　**T**　　**F**

2. In this passage, the word **horizontal** means:

    A. level with the ground

    B. far away from the ground

    C. in front of the ground

3. How can you tell that these monkey bars were built for children instead of adults?

_____

_____

4. Do you think that arm strength or leg strength is more important for playing on monkey bars? Why?

_____

_____

■ Choose one extension activity.

    A. Design your own monkey bars. Draw what your monkey bars look like. How are they different from regular monkey bars? How would you play on them?

    B. Think about the term "monkey bars." Make a list of three new names for this type of playground equipment. Explain why each one would be a better choice.

A FOOT SANDWICH

■ Read the passage.
Fastest Sandwich Made Using Feet,
November 10, 2000

There are many Guinness World Records™ records that are a bit **zany**. The record that Rob Williams (USA) set in 2000 has to be one of them. He made a sandwich using just his feet. He made it with **bologna**, cheese, and lettuce. He even added olives on little sticks. How long did it take him? He finished making the sandwich in 1 minute, 57 seconds.

DID YOU KNOW?
This three-man show lasted 20 years from 1984 to 2004. Since then, Williams has continued to perform his act at a fair in Ohio. "I just love it," he said. First, he makes a sandwich. Then, he serves it to someone in the audience.

Williams turned his unusual trick into a show. He joined two other men. Together, they toured the world. The show, called "What Goes Up," was funny. The actors did all sorts of crazy stunts on stage. They juggled pins and rings. They cut paper to bits with a whip. They joked with the audience.

Williams's act drew some of the biggest laughs. First, he washed and dried his feet. Then, he took bread from a bag. He added a slice of meat along with a slice of cheese. Next, he added a pickle. Finally, he squirted on some mustard. All of this was done with just his feet. Now, there is just one question. Would you eat a sandwich made by someone's feet?

■ Answer the questions.

1. Circle *T* for true or *F* for false.

Rob Williams set a world record for eating a
sandwich while holding it only with his feet.   **T   F**

2. As used in this passage, **bologna** is:
-   **A.** a city in Italy
-   **B.** something ridiculous
-   **C.** a kind of smoked meat

3. What does **zany** mean? Give an example of something that is zany.

_____

_____

4. The author asks if you would eat a sandwich made by someone's feet. This suggests that
-   **A.** not many people eat sandwiches anymore.
-   **B.** many people might not want to eat a sandwich made by feet.
-   **C.** no one can really make a sandwich using only his or her feet.

5. Do you think Rob Williams is happy about his ability? Why or why not?

_____

_____

6. If you were asked to perform a funny stunt on stage, what would you do? Explain.

_____

_____

■ Choose one extension activity.
-   **A.** Research the history of sandwiches. Write a paragraph about what you learn.
-   **B.** People in different countries have different ideas about the polite way
    to eat. Choose a country and learn about the table manners there.

MORE THAN A MEAL

■ Read the passage.

Largest Hamburger Commercially Available, May 30, 2009

Many restaurants serve hamburgers in different sizes. There are double burgers. There are triple burgers. Sometimes burgers are sold by weight. There are quarter-pound burgers. There are even half-pound burgers. None of these comes close to the one that Mike Matkin made. His Guinness World Records™ record hamburger weighed 185.5 pounds (84.14 kg). That is about as much as a grown man. The burger is on the menu at Mallie's restaurant. If you want to buy one, it will cost you $499!

This is not the first time Mallie's has set the hamburger record. This restaurant did it once before. That time the burger was 164.8 pounds (74.75 kg). It cost only $399! This new record beats the old one by 20 pounds (9 kg).

How do you make a burger this big? First, Mallie's **sculpts** the meat into a patty. Second, it has to go in the oven. It takes three men to lift it. The burger cooks for 16 hours. Then, they let it cool. That takes another 8 hours. Next, it's covered with lettuce, tomatoes, and onions. They put on some bacon. They also add cheese and pickles. At last, they put the whole thing on a huge bun. To order this burger, you have to give Mallie's 72 hours notice. On their menu, it says, "There is ABSOLUTELY no reason for this burger. But, if you order it, we'll make it, and you figure out what to do with it!"

Name_____ Date_____

■ Answer the questions.

1. Mallie's record-breaking burger costs _____ .

2. How does Mallie's prepare the burger after it is cooked?

   _____

   _____

3. In this passage, the word **sculpts** means:

   A. shapes

   B. grinds

   C. cooks

4. What do you think Mallie's menu means when it says that there is "ABSOLUTELY no reason for this burger"?

   _____

   _____

5. If you owned a restaurant, what unusual item would you put on the menu to attract customers? Explain why you think your item would bring in business.

   _____

   _____

■ Choose one statement. Then, explain why you agree or disagree.

A. Mallie's giant burger is wasteful.

B. Mallie's burger will encourage healthy eating.

C. Mallie's has set a fair price for this burger.

PAPER DOLLS AND MORE PAPER DOLLS

■ Read the passage.
Longest Chain of Paper Dolls, June 10, 2009

In 2008, a French magazine wanted to break a record. It hoped to make the world's longest chain of paper dolls. The magazine asked its young readers for help. It printed a chain of 10 dolls. Children were asked to color the dolls and send them back. Many children responded. Some mailed back the chain of 10 dolls. Others copied the chain. They sent back many chains. A 12-year-old boy named Dylan sent in the most. He sent 400 chains. It took him six months to do them all. Thanks to all of the children, the magazine reached its goal. It set the record. It made a paper doll chain that was 2,591.83 feet (789.989 m) long. The chain had 20,000 dolls.

The children had fun setting the record. The project was more than just fun, however. It also served a good cause. It raised money. Money was **donated** for every doll chain that children sent in. In all, the project raised about $10,000. The money was used to build libraries in Vietnam. Children learned the power of working together. They also learned that they could have fun and do something to help others at the same time.

DID YOU KNOW?

Godey's Lady Book was the first American magazine to print a paper doll. The year was 1859. The paper doll was printed in black and white. There were also pages of costumes. The children could color the costumes and put them on the doll. Godey's never printed another paper doll. Many other magazines did, however. Today, children still have fun with paper dolls.

Name_____ Date_____

■ Answer the questions.

1. How did Dylan help in setting this record?

_____

_____

2. What were the children asked to do before sending in the paper doll chains?

_____

_____

3. What does the word **donated** mean? What else besides money can be donated?

_____

_____

4. The magazine that set this record was probably a

    A. science magazine.

    B. children's magazine.

    C. magazine about cars.

5. Would the magazine have set a world record without the help of children? Explain your answer.

_____

_____

6. If you had $10,000 to give to some special cause, what cause would you choose and why?

_____

_____

■ Choose one extension activity.

A. The magazine was in France, and the libraries built with the money were in Vietnam. Find France and Vietnam on a map. Discover three facts about each country.

B. Research to find out more about the history of paper dolls.

© Carson-Dellosa

REVIEW: WILD, WACKY & WEIRD

■ **Use the clues to complete the crossword puzzle. Choose your answers from the word bank.**

astronomical	horizontal	percent
bologna	injured	sculpts
donated	knack	witnesses
graphite	logo	zany

ACROSS

1. a kind of smoked meat
6. used in the lead of a pencil
8. level with the ground
9. clownish
10. shapes something
12. hurt

DOWN

2. very large
3. a part out of one hundred
4. people who see something happen
5. a talent for something
7. given to a cause
11. a symbol that identifies a company or product

REVIEW: WILD, WACKY & WEIRD

■ Match the descriptions on the left with the items on the right.

_____ 1. Mallie's Restaurant charges $499 for this giant one. **A.** pencil

_____ 2. Rob Williams (USA) made this using only his feet. **B.** chocolate rabbit

_____ 3. Ken Courtney (USA) made the most
 expensive ones. **C.** car

_____ 4. Ashrita Furman (USA) made one as long as a
 tennis court. **D.** monkey bars

_____ 5. A company made a giant one to celebrate
 its 60th anniversary. **E.** ice cream cup

_____ 6. Lee Redmond (USA) broke hers in a car accident. **F.** fingernails

_____ 7. A company in Brazil made the largest one. **G.** sandwich

_____ 8. Chad Fell (USA) made the largest one ever
 without using his hands. **H.** sneakers

_____ 9. John Evans (United Kingdom) balances this
 on his head. **I.** bubblegum bubble

_____ 10. A French magazine asked children to help
 make this. **J.** hamburger

_____ 11. There is a set in Japan that is longer than a
 football field. **K.** chain of paper dolls

ANSWER KEY

Page 11

1. F; 2. Answers will vary. 3. B; 4. A; 5. no, Answers will vary.

Page 13

1. T; 2. C; 3. eating up greedily, Answers will vary. 4. Answers will vary but may include the spider's prey. 5. Answers will vary.

Page 15

1. T; 2. bottom jaw; 3. A mammal is an animal that has hair, a backbone, and the ability to produce milk. Answers will vary. 4. Herbivores are animals that eat plants. Answers will vary. 5. Hippos eat grass found along riverbanks.

Page 17

1. ears; 2. rabbit homes, yes; 3. Answers will vary. 4. Answers will vary.

Page 19

1. T; 2. scientist; 3. C; 4. reacted, Answers will vary. 5. Answers will vary. 6. Answers will vary.

Page 21

1. F; 2. B; 3. to grow up, no; 4. C; 5. Answers will vary but may include that she is the smallest horse on record, overcame weakness as a newborn, gets along with the animals on the farm, sleeps in a doghouse, and is great with children. 6. Answers will vary.

Page 23

1. post office; 2. to die out, Answers will vary. 3. Three times they have produced the Largest Egg from a Living Bird. 4. Answers will vary. 5. Answers will vary.

Page 25

1. vines, grass, and fruit; 2. F; 3. A; 4. Humans have hunted them. 5. Answers will vary. 6. Answers will vary.

Page 27

1. A; 2. T; 3. meat; 4. Answers will vary. 5. Answers will vary.

Page 29

1. C; 2. F; 3. to pass on information to others, Answers will vary. 4. by making sounds such as whistles and by moving their bodies (flapping their flippers, or jumping out of the water); 5. Answers will vary. 6. Answers will vary but may include breathe, move, cough, sneeze, dream. Some people also talk and walk in their sleep.

Page 31

1. T; 2. Answers will vary but may include size of the tank, age of the fish, and amount of food available. 3. set up, Answers will vary. 4. Answers will vary. 5. Answers will vary.

Page 33

1. Africa; 2. T; 3. A; 4. Beetles help keep the earth clean by eating leaves and waste matter. 5. Answers will vary but may include that beetles would be more vulnerable without their shells and less able to live in extreme conditions.

Page 35

1. T; 2. Most Jumps with a Jump Rope in One Minute; 3. to show devotion or attention over time, Answers will vary. 4. She is famous because 13 million people saw her do her amazing tricks on TV. 5. A

Page 36

v	a	m	m	e	d	e	v	o	u	r	i	n	g	s
e	g	a	x	l	e	s	p	e	x	o	c	a	c	d
g	h	p	i	p	d	e	l	i	c	a	t	e	y	v
e	u	d	q	g	i	t	r	n	i	m	n	e	n	w
t	r	a	r	n	c	o	x	o	p	i	i	x	a	g
a	e	d	e	m	a	t	u	r	e	d	o	t	d	u
r	g	a	e	a	t	d	v	e	d	a	r	i	t	u
i	e	p	v	a	i	n	c	o	m	u	n	d	r	s
a	m	t	b	n	o	a	p	r	a	r	h	c	a	p
n	r	c	r	a	n	k	s	e	m	a	a	t	a	e
i	a	e	d	e	v	o	a	m	m	v	o	x	c	c
e	s	t	a	b	l	i	s	h	a	a	s	t	p	i
n	t	e	h	u	t	c	h	i	l	p	h	v	e	e
d	a	c	o	m	m	u	n	i	c	a	t	e	s	s
e	c	a	v	e	g	r	e	s	p	o	n	d	e	d

Page 37

1. ostrich; 2. tortoise; 3. hippo; 4. dolphin; 5. giraffe; 6. goldfish; 7. dog; 8. horses

Page 39

1. 13; 2. C; 3. what you eat, Answers will vary. 4. Answers will vary.

Page 41

1. 10 feet (3 m) tall; 2. B; 3. Answers will vary. 4. Answers will vary. 5. Answers will vary. 6. Answers will vary but may include a spacecraft or tree fort.

Page 43

1. They are dying off. 2. B; 3. places where an animal normally lives, Answers will vary. 4. Answers will vary. 5. Humans can destroy animal habitats by taking over more land and restore or enlarge them by returning land to the wild and by setting up artificial habitats or feeding stations.

Page 45

1. A; 2. T; 3. Without collagen, the body would fall apart. Answers will vary. 4. to fasten together, Answers will vary. 5. Answers will vary.

Page 47

1. swimming; 2. A; 3. the act or process of competing, Answers will vary. 4. Answers will vary but may include how the eye would react to certain liquids.

Page 49

1. T; 2. Largest Dome; 3. A; 4. Answers will vary but should include how difficult it would be to construct this type of building. 5. In the winter, the weather in Canada is cold enough that ice does not melt.

Page 51

1. F; 2. They slide along it, and they use it to stick to various surfaces. 3. Answers will vary but may include danger, menace, risk, or hazard. 4. B; 5. Answers will vary.

Page 53

1. mother, friends, and neighbors; 2. house, garage, museum; 3. measurement around a circle, Answers will vary. 4. Answers will vary. 5. Answers will vary but should include that the ball was created by a child.

Page 55

1. F; 2. walking sticks; 3. A; 4. Answers will vary but may include that the removal of the tumor at age 10 would have prevented him from growing so tall. 5. Answers will vary.

Page 56

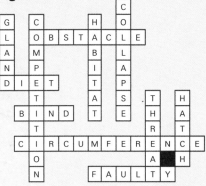

Page 57

eye; Largest; hair; Skin; Tallest; Snail; Truck; Bird Feeder; Plastic Wrap

Page 59

1. B; 2. cloth or wool, Answers will vary. 3. Answers will vary. 4. A; 5. Answers will vary.

Page 61

1. watermelon; 2. Answers will vary. 3. C; 4. material used to make something, Answers will vary. 5. Answers will vary.

Page 63

1. T; 2. B; 3. to stand straight up from the ground, Answers will vary. 4. Answers will vary but may include that it was steep and slippery. 5. Answers will vary.

Page 65

1. B; 2. Answers will vary but may include knives, arrows, water pipes, chairs, wind chimes, fishing poles, bridges, and homes. 3. hot and humid, Answers will vary. 4. Answers will vary but may include to emphasize that bamboo is an excellent building material.

Page 67

1. F; 2. China; 3. poisonous, Answers will vary. 4. produces, Answers will vary. 5. A; 6. Answers will vary.

Page 69

1. F; 2. C; 3. relating to the moon; 4. Answers will vary. 5. Answers will vary.

Page 71

1. F; 2. A; 3. Answers will vary but should include sloppy and uneven, not a normal web. 4. Arabella's web was poorly made; it took the spiders days to begin spinning more normal webs; and both spiders died. 5. Answers will vary.

Page 73

1. good luck; 2. Answers should be three of the following: Clover is a deep green color, soft to walk on, easy to mow, and easy to maintain, or four-leaf clovers are a sign of luck. 3. B; 4. Answers will vary. 5. Answers will vary.

Page 75

1. B; 2. T; 3. large and heavy, Answers will vary. 4. Answers will vary. 5. Answers will vary.

Page 77

1. A; 2. bathrooms, bedrooms, nurseries for babies; 3. animals that eat other animals, Answers will vary. 4. Answers will vary but may include that prairie dogs live in communities, or towns, so it appears they prefer company over solitude.

Page 79

1. T; 2. Answers should be two of the following: hoppity hop, bouncer, or kangaroo ball. 3. deserving of attention, Answers will vary. 4. Answers will vary. 5. Answers will vary.

Page 80

1. lunar; 2. noteworthy; 3. fleece; 4. omit; 5. tropical; 6. predators; 7. massive; 8. relieve; 9. toxic; 10. orbit; 11. ingredient; 12. vertical; 13. yields; RECORD SETTERS

Page 81

1. H; 2. K; 3. A; 4. B; 5. D; 6. F; 7. E; 8. J; 9. I; 10. G; 11. C

Page 83

1. F; 2. C; 3. Answers will vary but may include reality, fact, or truth. 4. Answers will vary but may include horseback riding (horse), cycling (bike), or skiing (skis). 5. Answers will vary.

Page 85

1. T; 2. C; 3. Answers will vary. 4. Answers will vary. 5. Answers will vary.

Page 87

1. F; 2. so that wind will not blow down his card house; 3. A; 4. Answers will vary. 5. Answers will vary. 6. Answers will vary.

Page 89

1. charity; 2. to breathe underwater; 3. C; 4. mud pools, large rocks, and slope; 5. Answers will vary.

Page 91

1. F; 2. were a part of; 3. Answers will vary. 4. Although she knew how to walk on stilts, she saw running on them as "a new challenge." She fell several times while training for the race. 5. Answers will vary.

Page 93

1. T; 2. two layers of fur; 3. B; 4. No, because they have lots of energy and enjoy cold weather. 5. Answers will vary.

Page 95

1. T; 2. C; 3. Answers will vary. 4. Answers will vary.

Page 97

1. F; 2. telephone poles; 3. lacking a definite plan or pattern, Answers will vary. 4. Answers will vary. 5. Answers will vary. 6. Answers will vary.

Page 99

1. steering and braking; 2. catchy saying; The sledding slogan reminds people that sledding can be risky. 3. It is easy to carry up a hill. 4. Answers will vary. 5. Answers will vary. The phrase lets people know that this sled is safe and easy for everyone to use, and that no one is too old to use it.

Page 100

p	a	u	t	i	d	d	r	a	l	m	e
t	y	g	a	f	e	g	m	a	c	o	c
r	e	n	n	d	s	l	o	r	e	m	o
p	a	r	t	i	c	i	p	a	t	e	n
u	s	a	u	n	e	f	a	n	i	n	s
m	i	s	c	e	n	e	r	d	u	t	t
o	e	l	o	n	d	p	a	o	g	m	r
s	c	o	u	t	e	r	y	m	e	m	u
o	r	g	d	e	d	i	p	a	n	n	c
m	u	a	t	p	a	u	y	c	s	e	t
r	e	n	i	r	u	n	n	e	r	s	e
t	f	a	n	t	a	s	y	r	n	n	d
c	o	u	l	a	g	a	s	d	e	t	a

Page 101

bike; marathon; nose; Largest; giant; bike; dance; faster; Cards

Page 103

1. They are dipped in gold. 2. C;
3. enormously large, Answers will vary.
4. A; 5. Answers will vary. 6. Answers
will vary.

Page 105

1. A; 2. T; 3. A; 4. Answers will vary.
5. Answers will vary.

Page 107

1. to celebrate their 60th anniversary;
2. vanilla; 3. made sure something was
correct. It is important to confirm a
record so that everyone will know it is
accurate. 4. Answers will vary. 5. No,
Answers will vary.

Page 109

1. cut her nails on live TV; 2. she was
hurt, in a car accident; 3. She soaked
them in olive oil and cleaned them with
a toothbrush. 4. Answers will vary.
5. Answers will vary.

Page 111

1. Germany; 2. F; 3. A; 4. Answers will
vary. 5. Answers will vary.

Page 113

1. T; 2. Answers should include two of
the following: longest pencil, greatest
Guinness World Records record-breaker,
biggest lollipop, farthest underwater
pogo stick travel, or Hula-hoop® racing
while balancing a milk bottle on his
head. 3. the center of the pencil, which
is the part that writes; 4. Answers will
vary. 5. Answers will vary.

Page 115

1. "Bubble Man"; 2. people who watch
something happen, Answers will vary.
3. A; 4. producing the bubble on film,
having witnesses, using no more than
three pieces of gum, holding the bubble
for five seconds, and not touching the
bubble with his hands; 5. Answers will
vary. 6. Answers will vary.

Page 117

1. F; 2. A; 3. The monkey bars are not
tall enough for adults to use. 4. arm
strength, Answers will vary.

Page 119

1. F; 2. C; 3. wacky, Answers will vary.
4. B; 5. Answers will vary.
6. Answers will vary.

Page 121

1. $499; 2. They cover it with lettuce,
tomato, onions, bacon, cheese and
pickles, and then put it on a giant bun.
3. A; 4. Answers will vary.
5. Answers will vary.

Page 123

1. He made 400 paper doll chains.
2. color them; 3. given away, Answers
will vary. 4. B; 5. no, Answers will vary.
6. Answers will vary.

Page 124

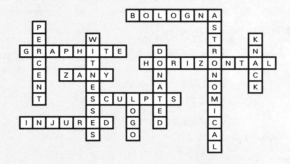

Page 125

1. J; 2. G; 3. H; 4. A; 5. E; 6. F; 7. B; 8. I;
9. C; 10. K; 11. D